Change Your Thoughts, Change Your Life.

Using the power of your mind to create your ideal life.

Change Your Thoughts, Change Your Life.

Using the power of your mind
to create your ideal life.

William Walker Atkinson

Originally published in 1906 as:

*"Thought Vibration;
Or, the Law of Attraction in the Thought World"*

Editing and Commentary by
Irene McGarvie

Ancient Wisdom Publishing
a division of Nixon-Carre Ltd., Toronto, ON

Library and Archives Canada Cataloguing in Publication

Atkinson, William Walker, 1862-1932
    Change your thoughts, change your life : using
the power of your mind to create your ideal life / William
Walker Atkinson ; edited by Irene McGarvie.

Updated version of: Thought vibration, or, The law of
attraction in the thought world.
ISBN 978-1-926826-03-5

    1. New Thought. 2. Mind and body. I. McGarvie,
Irene, 1957- II. Title.

BF639.A83 2011   158.1
C2011-900629-4

Published by:
**Ancient Wisdom Publishing
A division of Nixon-Carre Ltd.
P.O. Box 92533, Carlton RPO
Toronto, Ontario, M5A 4N9**

**www.learnancientwisdom.com
www.nixon-carre.com**

**Distributed by Ingram 1-800-937-8000
www.ingrambook.com**

Printed and bound in the USA

Contents

"No one saves us but ourselves.
No one can and no one may.
We ourselves must walk the path."

Buddha

Preface

Don't Follow Me

I received a letter from an earnest student of New Thought, who writes me that he is endeavoring to put into practice my teachings. That is all right - I think he will get some good out of the practice (I know that I do). But here is where the trouble comes in - he goes on to say that he is "a faithful disciple" of mine, and is content to "sit at the feet of the Teacher." I don't want any "disciples" - disciples are mere parrots repeating what one says - mere human sheep trotting along after some conceited old bellwether.

I want every one of my fellow students of Mental Science to be his own bellwether. I like comradeship and mutual help - the help of interdependence. But I don't like this talk of master and disciple - of leader and follower - this talk and idea of dependence.

As for sitting at anyone's feet, I don't sit at anyone's feet and I don't want anyone to sit at mine. I am willing, and often glad, to listen to some teacher and to pick from his teachings such bits of truth as my mind is ready to receive. I am willing to say "I don't know," and to accept from others that which appeals to me as truth; not because the other says that it is truth, but because my mind recognizes it as such. I take my own wherever I find it, because I recognize it as mine. I know that all students and teachers get their knowledge from the only source of supply - they can't get it from anywhere else.

If some other fellow happens to see a particular bit of truth before I do, I gladly accept a portion of it from his hand, be he king or beggar, while if I happen to see the thing first, I will gladly share it with all who may want it. We are all fellow students - that's all. I recognize no man as my master and I spurn the person who would call me "Master," if there be any so foolish.

I am fully aware that certain teachers convey the idea that they are chosen mouthpieces of the Infinite and that all true teachings must bear their hallmark. I also know the fanatical devotion and bigotry that many of the followers of such teachers manifest. But this is all folly, these teachers sooner or later will be shown up to be no wiser or better than anyone else, and the "disciples" will be made to stand upon their own feet, by reason of the props being knocked out from under them. The New Thought movement aims at making individuals, not at converting people into droves of sheep following the tinkle of the bell of some conceited leader.

The growing soul must realize that it has within itself all that it requires. It may gladly accept from others suggestions, advice, bits of knowledge, and the like, as it goes along - the soul itself being the only judge of what it requires at each particular stage. But, in the end, it must do its own work, and must stand on its own feet. All the teachings in the world will not help you, unless you take hold of the matter yourself. You cannot get true mental or spiritual teaching by paying so much for a course of lessons, and doing nothing yourself. You must bring something to the table before you can take anything away. You must work up to an understanding before the teachings of another will do you any good. The teacher may make a suggestion that will open up a line of thought for you, or he many point out a way that has proved of value to him; and thus save you much time and trouble. But you must do the work yourself.

A teacher may be so filled with the truth that he will overflow and you will get some of the overflow. I believe that truth is "catching." But even so, unless you make that truth your own by living it out, and applying it to your needs, it will do you no good. So long as you are content to "sit at his feet," and act as a "disciple" you will not grow one inch. You will be merely a reflection of the teacher, instead of being an individual.

We need reminding of this every once in a while, "lest we forget." It is so easy to have your thoughts predigested for you by some teacher or writer, so easy to receive your teachings in capsules. It is so nice to be able to sit down and swallow the tablet that the teacher or writer kindly has prepared for you, and imagine that you are getting the real thing. But I tell you, friends - it won't work. Imbibe all the teachings you please, but you have got to get down to business yourself. You can't give someone else a power of attorney to do the work in your place. Life accepts no substitutes - you must step out yourself. It is mighty easy - this idea of paying so much, in time or money, to some teacher or writer, and then sneaking into the Kingdom of Heaven holding on to his skirt - but it won't work. You have got to do some hustling on your own account, and don't you make any mistake about this fact.

Many of you are running around after teachers, preachers, prophets, seers, "illuminated souls," and what not, expecting that your little fee for courses of lessons, private teachings, and all the rest, is going to land you right up in the front rank. Don't you believe a word of it, you have to go through the motions yourself, before you will attain anything. You can't sneak in that way - it won't work.

I look around and see many of these poor creatures "sitting at the feet" of someone or other, sinking their individuality into that of the teacher, and not daring to think an original thought - lest it conflict with some notion of their "Master." These good souls are so full of the teaching they are imbibing, they will repeat it by the yard, phrase after phrase, like a well-trained parrot. But they don't understand a bit of it. They are like the moon which shines by reason of a reflection of the sun's rays, but has no light or heat of its own. Stop this moon business and build yourself into a sun. You have it in you - manifest it. Start yourself in motion and manifest Life.

Don't suppose that you must be able to solve all the riddles of the universe before you can do anything. Never mind about those riddles, just get down to the task that lies ahead of you, just get down to business and begin to live.

Don't make the mistake of supposing that this or that teacher has solved the Great Riddle. If he says that he has, he is only bluffing and whistling to keep up courage. He may have found a good-sized chunk of the truth, and if he is willing to pass you a bit of it, all right, but he hasn't the Whole Thing, not by a mighty sight. The Whole Thing isn't placing itself in the exclusive control of any little bit of itself. No one has a monopoly of knowing - a corner on the Truth. It is yours as much as anybody's - but you must dig for it.

Sometimes I amuse myself by reading some of the theories and "explanations" of those who think that they have hold of the Whole Thing. After I get through with the theories of one "dead-sure" chap, I take up the directly opposite theories of another fellow who considers himself the special mouthpiece of the Absolute. Reading all this can get confusing, but when I get worked up over such things I go out into the sun and fall back on the "Laughing Philosophy," which soon brings me around all right. Nothing will puncture these bubbles so quickly as a good dose of Laughter. Laughter is the only thing that keeps us from madness. The sense of humor is God's best gift to man.

Beware of any teachings that will not stand the test of the sunny out-of-doors, and the application of the Laughing Philosophy. Shun the teachings that require a pursed-up mouth, and a strained, sober face. Have nothing to do with teachings that require a dim, dark, sunless room to be absorbed in. Carry out into the sun the teachings that are offered you, and see whether or not they fade. Apply the chemical of laughter, and determine whether the stuff bleaches. Remember this test when you are perplexed or worried over some strange theory or doctrine, no matter where it comes from. If anyone tells you something which will not bear the test, discard the teaching. Try this on my writings as well as the others.

Stop being moons. Stop living by reflected light. Get into action and convert yourself into a living sun. You can do it. It is within your power. Every human soul contains within it the elements of the Sun - get to work and express yourself. Stiffen up your backbone and hold your head erect. Don't be afraid to say "I am IT."

So don't tell me that you are "disciples" of mine - I disown you, I refuse to have disciples. But if you wish to call me "Brother," or "Fellow Student," or "Schoolmate in the Kindergarten of God," I will be glad to have you do so. That's all we are, after all, little babes tugging away at the breast of the Absolute.

William Walker Atkinson
1906

"All that we are is the result of what we have thought."

Buddha

The Law of Attraction 1

The universe is governed by laws

Nothing happens by accident, nothing occurs as a result of luck or magic. We are familiar with some of the laws of the universe, but are almost totally ignorant of the others. We are learning a little more every day -- our veil of ignorance is gradually being lifted.

We know all about the Law of Gravity, but most of us are totally unaware of another important law, the Law of Attraction in the Thought World. We are familiar with the law which draws and holds together the atoms which make up matter. We recognize the power of the law that attracts bodies to the earth, and that holds the circling worlds in their places, but we are ignorant of the mighty law that draws to us the things we desire or fear. This is the law that makes or mars our lives.

When we come to realize that our thoughts are a force, a manifestation of energy which has a magnet-like power of attraction, we begin to understand many things that have up until now made no apparent sense to us. There is no other study that will repay the student for his time and trouble as well as the study of the workings of this mighty law, the Law of Attraction in the Thought World.

What is Natural Law?

When something happens and we don't understand the cause people sometimes attribute supernatural causes. But in reality, nothing is supernatural, if something seems supernatural it just means that we don't understand the natural reason for it. Our universe is governed by laws, Atkinson mentions the law of gravity because everyone is familiar with it. We all know that if we drop something gravity will cause it to fall toward the floor. Basically, the Natural Law that Atkinson is talking about involves cause and effect, if we do this then that will happen. In this chapter he is saying that if we think in specific ways then specific things will happen.

This should not be confused with what is referred to as Natural Law in legal philosophy which is about ethics, and social behavior and the justification for man-made laws.

Our thoughts are vibrations

When we think we send out vibrations which are as real as the vibrations of light, heat, electricity, and magnetism. That these vibrations are not evident to our five senses is no proof that they do not exist. A powerful magnet will send out vibrations and exert a force sufficient to attract to itself a piece of steel weighing hundreds of pounds, but we can neither see, taste, smell, hear nor feel the mighty force.

Our thought vibrations, likewise, cannot be seen, tasted, smelled, heard nor felt in the ordinary way. Although it is true there are some people who are particularly sensitive to psychic impressions who have perceived powerful thought-waves, and very many of us can testify that at times we have distinctly felt the thought vibrations of others, both whilst in the presence of the sender and at a distance, most of the time the power of our thought waves goes unnoticed.

Light and heat are manifested by vibrations of a far lower intensity than those of thought, but the difference is solely in the rate of vibration.

As scientist Elisha Gray says in his book, "The Miracles of Nature":

"There is much food for speculation in the thought that there exist sound-waves that no human ear can hear, and color-waves of light that no eye can see. The long, dark, soundless space between 40,000 and 400,000,000,000,000 vibrations per second, and the infinity of range beyond 700,000,000,000,000 vibrations per second, where light ceases, in the universe of motion, makes it possible to indulge in speculation."

M. M. Williams, in his work entitled "Short Chapters in Science," says:

"There is no gradation between the most rapid undulations or tremblings that produce our sensation of sound, and the slowest of those which give rise to our sensations of gentlest warmth. There is a huge gap between them, wide enough to include another world of motion, all lying between our world of sound and our world of heat and light; and there is no good reason whatever for supposing that matter is incapable of such intermediate activity, or that such activity may not give rise to intermediate sensations, provided there are organs for taking up and sensing their movements."

I cite the above authorities merely to give you food for thought, not to attempt to demonstrate to you the fact that thought vibrations exist. That fact has now been fully established to the satisfaction of numerous researchers, and if you think about it you will realize that it coincides with your own experiences.

Thoughts are things

We often hear repeated the well-known Science of Mind statement, "Thoughts are Things," and we say these words over and over without consciously realizing just what the statement means. If we fully comprehended the truth of this statement and the natural consequences of the truth behind it, we would understand many things which we never understood before, and we would be able to use the wonderful power of Thought Force just as we use any other manifestation of Energy.

When we think we set into motion vibrations of a very high frequency, just as real as the vibrations of light, heat, sound, electricity. When we understand the laws governing the production and transmission of these vibrations we will be able to use them in our daily life, just as we do all the other, better known, forms of energy. That we cannot see, hear, weigh or measure these vibrations is no proof that they do not exist. There exist waves of sound which no human ear can hear, although some of these are undoubtedly registered in the ear of insects or other animals, and others are caught by delicate scientific instruments invented by man.

As new instruments are invented, new vibrations are recorded by them - and yet the vibrations were just as real before the invention of the instrument as afterward. Supposing that we had no instruments to register magnetism - one might be justified in denying the existence of that mighty force, because it could not be tasted, felt, smelt, heard, seen, weighed or measured, and yet the mighty magnet would still send out waves sufficient to draw to it pieces of steel weighing hundreds of pounds.

Thoughts attract thoughts

We are sending out thoughts of greater or less intensity all the time, and we are reaping the results of such thoughts. Not only do our thought-waves influence ourselves and others, but they have a drawing power - they attract to us the thoughts of others, things, circumstances, people, "luck," in accord with the character of the thought uppermost in our minds.

Thoughts of Love will attract to us the Love of others; circumstances and surroundings in accord with the thought, and people who are of like thought. Thoughts of Anger, Hate, Envy, Malice and Jealousy will draw to us the foul brood of kindred thoughts emanating from the minds of others; circumstances in which we will be called upon to manifest these vile thoughts and will receive them in turn from others. We will draw to ourselves people who will manifest disharmony.

A strong thought, or a thought long continued, will make us the center of attraction for the corresponding thought-waves of others. Like attracts like in the Thought World - as ye sow so shall ye reap. Birds of a feather flock together in the Thought World - curses like chickens come home to roost, and bring their friends with them.

The man or woman who is filled with Love sees Love on all sides and attracts the Love of others. The man with Hate in his heart gets all the Hate he can stand. The man who thinks Fight generally runs up against all the Fight he wants before he gets through. And so it goes, each gets what he calls for over the wireless telegraph of the Mind. The man who rises in the morning feeling "grumpy" usually manages to have the whole family in the same mood before the breakfast is over. The "nagging" woman generally finds enough to gratify her "nagging" propensity during the day.

The calm in the storm

This matter of Thought Attraction is a serious one. When you stop to think of it you will see that a man really makes his own surroundings, although he blames others for it. I have known people who understood this law to hold a positive, calm thought and be absolutely unaffected by the disharmony surrounding them. They rested safely and calmly while the tempest raged around them. One is not at the mercy of the fitful storms of Thought after he has learned the workings of the Law.

We have passed through the age of physical force on to the age of intellectual supremacy, and are now entering a new and almost unknown field, that of psychic power. This field of energy has its established laws, and we should acquaint ourselves with them. Once you understand these laws you will be able to make use of this great power and apply it for legitimate and worthy purposes. The results will amaze you.

Chapter 1 Summary

- Everything is governed by laws

- Our thoughts are vibrations

- Our thoughts attract other thoughts with similar vibrations

- We attract what we think about

Thought Waves

2

Ripples in an ocean of thought

Like a stone thrown into the water, thought produces ripples and waves which spread out over the great ocean of thought. There is this difference, however: the waves on the water move only on a level plane in all directions, whereas thought-waves move in all directions from a common center, just as do the rays from the sun.

Just as we here on earth are surrounded by a great sea of air, so are we surrounded by a great sea of Mind. Our thought-waves move through this vast mental ether, extending, in all directions, becoming somewhat lessened in intensity according to the distance traveled, because of the friction caused by the waves coming in contact with the great body of Mind surrounding us on all sides.

These thought-waves have other qualities

that differ from the waves on the water. They are able to reproduce themselves. In this respect they resemble sound-waves rather than waves upon the water. Just as a note of the violin will cause a thin glass to vibrate and "sing," so will a strong thought tend to awaken similar vibrations in minds attuned to receive it. Many of the "stray thoughts" which come to us are but reflections or answering vibrations to some strong thought sent out by another. But unless our minds are attuned to receive it, the thought will not likely affect us.

If we are thinking high and great thoughts, our minds acquire a certain keynote corresponding to the character of the thoughts we have been thinking. And, this keynote once established, we will be apt to catch the vibrations of other minds keyed to the same thought. On the other hand, if we get into the habit of thinking thoughts of an opposite character we will soon be echoing the low order of thought emanating from the minds of the thousands thinking along the same lines.

We are largely what we have thought ourselves into being, the balance being represented by the character of the suggestions and thought of others, which have reached us either directly by verbal suggestions or telepathically by means of thought-waves. Our general mental attitude, however, determines the character of the thought-waves received from others as well as the thoughts emanating from ourselves. We receive only such thoughts as are in harmony with the general mental attitude we hold; the thoughts not in harmony with our thoughts affect us very little, as they awaken no response in us.

Confidence and determination

The man who believes thoroughly in himself and maintains a positive strong mental attitude of Confidence and Determination is not likely to be affected by the adverse and negative thoughts of Discouragement and Failure emanating from the minds of other persons in whom these negative thoughts predominate. At the same time these negative thoughts, if they reach one whose mental attitude is pitched on a low key, deepen his negative state and add fuel to the fire which is consuming his strength, or, if you prefer this figure, serve to further smother the fire of his energy and activity.

We attract to us the thoughts of others of the same order of thought. The man who thinks success will be apt to get into tune with the minds of others thinking likewise, and they will help him, and he them. The man who allows his mind to dwell constantly upon thoughts of failure brings himself into close touch with the minds of other "failure" people, and each will tend to pull the other down still more. The man who thinks that all is evil is apt to see much evil, and will be brought into contact with others who will seem to prove his theory. And the man who looks for good in everything and everybody will be likely to attract to himself the things and people corresponding to his thought. We generally see what we look for.

Varying frequencies

You can understand this idea more clearly if you will think of a radio or a cell phone, which receives the vibrations only from a sending instrument which has been attuned to the same frequency, while other signals are passing through the air in near vicinity without affecting them.

The same law applies to the operations of our thought. We receive only that which corresponds to our mental attunement, our mental frequency. If we are discouraged, we may rest assured that we have dropped into a negative frequency, and have been affected not only by our own thoughts but have also received the added depressing thoughts of similar character which are constantly being sent out from the minds of other unfortunate people who have not yet learned the law of attraction in the thought world. Correspondingly, if we occasionally rise to heights of enthusiasm and energy, how quickly we feel the inflow of the courageous, daring, energetic, positive thoughts being sent out by other enthusiastic men and women of the world. We recognize this without much trouble when we come in personal contact with people and feel their vibrations, depressing or invigorating, as the case may be. But the same law operates when we are not in their presence, although less strongly.

The mind has many degrees of pitch, ranging from the highest positive note to the lowest negative note, with many notes in between, varying in pitch according to their respective distance from the positive or negative extreme.

When your mind is operating along positive lines you feel strong, buoyant, bright, cheerful, happy, confident and courageous, and are able to do your work well, to carry out your intentions, and progress on your road to Success. You send out strong positive thought, which affects others and causes them to co-operate with you or to follow your lead, according to their own mental keynote.

When you are playing on the extreme negative end of the mental keyboard you feel depressed, weak, passive, dull, fearful, and cowardly. You find yourself unable to make progress or to succeed. Your effect upon others is practically nil. You are led by, rather than leading others, and are used as a human door-mat or football.

Positive or negative interactions with others

In some persons the positive element seems to predominate, and in others the negative quality seems to be more in evidence. There are, of course, widely varying degrees of positiveness and negativeness, and B may be negative to A, while positive to C.

When two people first meet there is generally a silent mental conflict in which their respective minds test their quality of positiveness, and fix their relative position toward each other. This process may be unconscious in many cases, but it occurs nevertheless. The adjustment is often automatic, but occasionally the struggle is so sharp, the opponents being so well matched, that the matter forces itself into the consciousness of the two people. Sometimes both parties are so much alike in their degrees of positiveness that they practically fail to come to terms, mentally; they never really are able to get along with each other, and they are either mutually repelled and separate or else stay together amid constant strife and wrangling.

We are positive or negative to every one with whom we have relations. We may be positive to our children, our employees and our dependents, but we are at the same time negative to others to whom we occupy inferior positions, or whom we have allowed to assert themselves over us.

Of course, something may occur and we will suddenly become more positive than the man or woman to whom we have heretofore been negative. We frequently see cases of this kind. As the knowledge of these mental laws becomes more general we will see many more instances of persons asserting themselves and making use of their new-found power.

But remember that you possess the power to raise the frequency of your mind to a positive pitch by an effort of the will, and, of course, it is equally true that you may allow yourself to drop into a low, negative frequency by carelessness or a weak will.

There are more people on the negative plane of thought than on the positive plane, and consequently there are more negative thought vibrations in operation in our mental atmosphere. But, happily for us, this is counterbalanced by the fact that a positive thought is infinitely more powerful than a negative one, and if by force of will we raise ourselves to a higher mental frequency we can shut out the depressing thoughts and take up the vibrations corresponding with our changed mental attitude.

Positive affirmations

This is one of the secrets behind affirmations and auto-suggestions. There is no particular merit in affirmations by themselves, but they serve a twofold purpose:

> 1) They tend to establish new mental attitudes within us and act wonderfully in the direction of character building.

> 2) They tend to raise the mental frequency so that we may get the benefit of the positive thought-waves of others on the same plane of thought.

Whether or not we believe in them, we are constantly making affirmations. The person who asserts that he can and will do a thing - and asserts it earnestly - develops the qualities conducive to doing that thing, and at the same time places his mind in the proper frequency to receive all the thought waves likely to help him in the doing. If, on the other hand, you say and feel that you are going to fail, you will choke and smother the thoughts coming from your subconscious which are intended to help you, and at the same time will place yourself in tune with the failure thought vibrations of the world, and there are plenty of those kind of thoughts floating around.

Émile Coué the father of positive affirmations

Émile Coué de Châtaigneraie (1857-1926) was a French psychologist and pharmacist who found that praising the effectiveness of a particular medication resulted in noticeable increases in the drug's effectiveness upon the patient. He discovered that many patients could cure themselves by replacing thoughts of illness with thoughts of being cured, and that repeating words enough times causes the subconscious to absorb them.

Do not allow yourselves to be affected by the adverse and negative thoughts of those around you. Rise to the upper chambers of your mental dwelling, and set your frequency to a high pitch, far above the vibrations on the lower planes of thought. Then you will not only be immune to their negative vibrations but will be in touch with the great body of strong positive thoughts coming from those of your own plane of development.

My aim is to direct and train you in the proper use of thought and will, that you may be able to strike the positive key at any moment you may feel it necessary. It is not necessary to strike the extreme note on all occasions. The better plan is to keep yourself in a comfortable key, without much strain, and to have the means at your command so that you can raise the pitch at once when the occasion demands. With this knowledge you will not be at the mercy of the old automatic action of the mind, but will have it under your own control.

Practice and gradual improvement

Developing the will is very much like developing a muscle, it is a matter of practice and gradual improvement. At first it is tiresome, but with each repetition one grows stronger until the new strength becomes real and permanent. Many of us have made ourselves positive under sudden calls or emergencies. We are in the habit of "bracing up" when occasion demands. But with practice you can be so much strengthened that your habitual state will be equal to your bracing up state now, and then when you find it necessary to apply the spur you will be able to reach a stage not yet dreamed of at present.

I am not advocating a state of high tension continuously. This is not desirable, not only because it is apt to be too much of a strain upon you, but also because you will find that you need to relieve the tension at times and will become receptive to lower/negative frequencies.

Chapter 2 Summary

• Our thought waves spread out through the air like ripples in water

• We are what we have thought ourselves into being

• You can choose to develop confidence and determination or remain stuck in discouragement and failure

• Our thoughts interact with the thoughts of others in either positive or negative ways

• Positive affirmations establish new mental attitudes within us

• Positive affirmations raise the mental frequency so that we can benefit from the positive thought-waves of others

*"Every day, in every way,
I'm getting better and better."*

**Émile Coué de Châtaigneraie
(1857-1926)**

The Mind

3

Active or passive effort

Our mind functions in response to one of two different kinds of mental effort, either active or passive. There are no obvious lines dividing the functions that are a result of active efforts and those that are a result of passive efforts. They often overlap similar to the way the colors of the spectrum fade into each other.

"Active" mental effort is the result of a deliberate thought.

"Passive" mental effort is the result of a preceding active mental effort which was produced internally or received externally from other sources.

The source of externally received thoughts could be someone else's active mental effort through suggestion, such as thought vibrations sent from one mind to another. These deliberate thoughts can also be inherited from ancestors and passed on through generations until the person has become sufficiently developed to activate these thoughts that are a result of active mental effort.

Active mental effort is freshly created while passive mental effort has its roots in past thought vibrations. Active mental effort creates its own path, like cutting a path with a machete in the jungle where none existed before, while passive mental effort follows the beaten path already opened by a previous active mental effort.

Active thoughts become habits

A thought or action, originated by an active mental effort, if repeated deliberately, becomes habitual, a passive mental effort which repeats continuously until it is stopped or changed by another deliberate active mental effort. In other words, repetitive thoughts or actions, which are the result of passive mental effort, can be changed or ended by active mental effort. Therefore, active mental effort creates, changes, or destroys thoughts and actions while passive mental effort obeys orders and suggestions.

Active mental effort transmits vibrations that

produce thoughts and actions which become habit-forming through passive mental effort. Active mental effort can also emit vibrations that neutralize the momentum of habitual thoughts and actions. Beyond that, it can emit vibrations that will be stronger than the passive mental effort that sustains the habit and replace the original habit with a new one.

All thoughts and actions, once activated, continue to vibrate due to passive mental effort until they are corrected or terminated by subsequent thought vibrations produced by active mental effort, or other controlling power. The longer thoughts and actions continue as habits, the more difficult it will be to correct or end them. This is what is meant by "force of habit." I think that anyone who has struggled to break a habit that was easily acquired will certainly understand. This Law applies to good habits as well as bad ones. The moral is obvious.

Thoughts and actions can be the result of the combination of several mental efforts. A task to be performed may call for the combined exercise of several mental efforts, some of which may be active mental efforts and others passive mental efforts.

Dealing with new problems and conditions requires active mental effort while familiar problems and tasks call upon passive mental effort.

Evolution

In Nature, living organisms instinctively act to satisfy their wants. The tendency to act this way is sometimes called Appetency. It is a passive mental effort stemming back to its original ancestor. As it passed from generation to generation, this survival instinct gained strength and power. The initial thought vibration of the first ancestor is amplified by the power of Universal Energy.

This tendency in plants is easily observable in simple plants as well as more elaborate ones. It is often called the "life force" of plants. It is a kind of rudimentary passive mental effort. In some higher forms of plant life, there is almost a sense of its own will. People who write about plants talk about many instances of this phenomenon which is obviously an example of active mental effort.

In the animal kingdom, a very high degree of passive mental effort is found. Depending on the species, a considerable amount of active mental effort is apparent. Animals undoubtedly are able to reason but to a lesser degree than Man. The amount of active mental effort displayed by animals is often as high as that shown by a child.

A child, before birth, shows in its body the stages of human physical evolution; a child, before and after birth, and until maturity, shows the stages of human mental evolution, Man, the highest form of life yet produced (at least in his own eyes), shows the highest form of passive mental effort, as well as a much higher development of active mental effort than is seen in the lower animals. The degree of active mental effort varies widely among different people. These varying degrees do not depend by any means on the social position or educational advantages possessed by the individual.

If you look around you will see the different stages of the development of active mental effort in Man. The reasoning of most people is scarcely more than passive mental effort, with little of the qualities of active mental effort. They prefer to let other people think for them. Active mental effort tires them and they find the instinctive, automatic, passive mental effort process much easier. Their minds work along the lines of least resistance. They are little more than human sheep.

Among both animals and men, active mental effort is largely confined to dealing with material needs. Active mental effort is used mostly to support instinctive, automatic passive mental effort.

As lower forms of life evolved, they developed new mental abilities which remained latent. These abilities at first always manifested in the form of rudimentary passive mental effort, but later developed into higher and higher forms of passive mental effort until finally acquiring the capacity for active mental effort. The evolutionary process strives to continually improve this capability for active mental effort.

This law of evolution is still in progress, and Man is beginning to develop new powers of mind, which, of course, are first manifesting themselves along the lines of passive mental effort. Some people have developed these new faculties to a considerable degree, and it is possible that before long mankind will be able to exercise them as active mental effort. In fact, this power has already been attained by a few.

I AM

The subjugation of the mind to the Will can be increased though proper practice. What is referred to as the "strengthening of the Will" is in reality the training of the mind to recognize and absorb the Power within. The Will is strong enough; it does not need strengthening, but the mind needs to be trained to receive and act on the suggestions of the Will. The Will is the outward manifestation of the "I AM."

The time of evolutionary development has

come when Man can help himself. The person who understands the Law can accomplish wonders by means of the development of the powers of the mind.

A person who understands the laws of their mental being can develop their latent powers and use them intelligently. This person does not despise their passive mental functions, but makes good use of them for which they are best fitted, and is able to obtain wonderful results from their work, having mastered them and trained them to do the bidding of the Higher Self. When these functions fail to do their work properly they regulate them, and their knowledge prevents them from meddling with them unintelligently, and thereby doing themselves any harm.

They develop the faculties and powers latent within themselves and learn how to manifest them using both active mental effort as well as passive mental effort. An individual knows that the real person within them is the master to whom both active mental effort and passive mental effort are but tools. They have banished Fear, and enjoy Freedom. They have found themselves. They have learned **THE SECRET OF THE "I AM."**

What does the author mean by "I AM?"

In the Bible, in Exodus 3:14, Moses asks God what his name is. God answers "I Am that I Am." In this chapter Atkinson is referring to the god, divinity, or creator inside of all of us. Whatever we say we are is what we are. For example, if you say "I am tired" then you are, or become, tired. In other words, we create our lives whenever we say I AM.

Chapter 3 Summary

• There are two kinds of thoughts, active and passive

• Active thoughts are the result of deliberate conscious effort

• Passive thoughts can be habits resulting from previous active thoughts

• Passive thoughts can be received from external sources

• All organisms are continuing to evolve

• A person who understands their thought processes understands the power within themselves

Mind Building

4

We can assert our will

We are all familiar with the concept of body building, but did you know that you can also build your mind? Man can build up his mind and make it what he wants it to be. In fact, we are mind-building every hour of our lives, either consciously or unconsciously. The majority of us are doing the work unconsciously, but those who have seen a little below the surface of things have taken the matter in hand and have become conscious creators of their own minds. They are no longer subject to the suggestions and influences of others but have become masters of their own minds. They assert the "I," and compel obedience from their minds.

The "I" is the sovereign of the mind, and what we call WILL is the instrument of the "I." Of course, there is something back of this, and the Universal Will is higher than the Will of the Individual, but the latter is in much closer touch with the Universal Will than is generally supposed, and when one conquers the lower self, and asserts the "I," he becomes in close touch with the Universal Will and has access to the wonderful power of the Universe. The moment one asserts the "I," and "finds himself," he establishes a close connection between the Individual Will and the Universal Will. But before he is able to avail himself of the mighty power at his command, he must first master his lower self.

Think of the absurdity of Man claiming to manifest powers, when he is the slave of his lower self. Think of a man being the slave of his moods, passions, animal appetites and lower faculties, and at the same time trying to claim the benefits of the Will. I am not preaching asceticism. I am speaking of Self-Mastery. All things are good when we learn to master them, but nothing is good when it masters us. Just so long as we allow the lower portions of the self to give us orders, we are slaves. It is only when the "I" mounts the throne and lifts the scepter, that order is established and things assume their proper relation to each other.

I am finding no fault with those who are swayed by their lower selves - they are in a lower place but will work their way up in time. Instead, I am calling the attention of those who are ready to evolve. It is time for your Sovereign mind to assert its will, and the subjects must obey. Orders must be given and carried out. Rebellion must be put down, and the rightful authority insisted upon. The time to do it is Now.

You have been allowing your rebellious subjects to keep the King from his throne. You have been allowing your mind to be misgoverned. You have been the slaves of Appetite, Unworthy Thoughts, Passion and Negative Thinking. The Will has been set aside and Low Desire has usurped the throne. It is time to re-establish order in the mental kingdom.

You are able to assert the mastery over any emotion, appetite, passion or class of thoughts by the assertion of the Will. You can order Fear to go to the rear; Jealousy to leave your presence; Hate to depart from your sight; Anger to hide itself; Worry to cease troubling you; Uncontrolled Appetite and Passion to bow in submission and to become humble slaves instead of masters - all by the assertion of the "I." You may surround yourself with the glorious company of Courage, Love and Self-Control, by the same means. You may put down the rebellion and secure peace and order in your mental kingdom if you will but utter the mandate and insist upon its execution. But before you march forth to victory, you must establish the proper internal conditions - you must show your ability to govern your own kingdom. The first battle is the conquest of the lesser self by the Real Self.

AFFIRMATION:

I Am Asserting the Mastery of My Real Self

Repeat these words earnestly and positively during the day, at least once an hour, and particularly when you are confronted with conditions which tempt you to act on the lines of the lesser self instead of following the course dictated by the Real Self.

In moments of doubt and hesitation, say these words earnestly, and your way will be made clear to you. Repeat them several times after you retire and settle yourself to sleep. But be sure to back up the words with the thought inspiring them, and do not merely repeat them parrot-like.

Form the mental image of the Real Self asserting its mastery over the lower planes of your mind - see the King on his Throne. You will become conscious of an influx of new thought, and things which have seemed hard for you will suddenly become much easier. You will feel that you have yourself well in hand, and that YOU are the master and not the slave. The thought you are holding will manifest itself in action, and you will steadily grow to become that which you have in mind.

EXERCISE:

Fix the mind firmly on the higher Self and draw inspiration from it when you feel led to yield to the promptings of the lower part of your nature. When you are tempted to burst into Anger assert the "I," and your voice will drop. Anger is unworthy of the developed Self. When you feel vexed and cross, remember what you are, and rise above your feeling.

When you feel Fearful, remember that the Real Self fears nothing, and assert Courage. When you feel Jealousy inciting, think of your higher nature, and laugh. And so on, asserting the Real Self and not allowing the things on the lower plane of mentality to disturb you. They are unworthy of you, and must be taught to keep their places. Do not allow these things to master you-they should be your subjects, not your masters. You must get away from this plane, and the only way to do so is to cut loose from these phases of thought which have been running things to suit themselves.

You may have trouble at the start, but keep at it and you will have that satisfaction which comes only from conquering the lower parts of our nature. You have been a slave long enough - now is the time to free yourselves. If you will follow these exercises faithfully you will be a different being by the end of the year, and will look back with a pitying smile to your former condition. But it takes work. This is not child's play, but a task for earnest men and women.

Will you make the effort?

Chapter 4 Summary

• We are always mind-building,
either consciously or unconsciously

• We have the power to control our will

• The Real Self inside us feels no fear
and is not jealous

5

The Secret of the Will

Will power can be developed with practice

While psychologists may differ in their theories regarding the nature of the Will, none deny its existence, nor question its power. All persons recognize the power of strong Will. All see how it may be used to overcome the greatest obstacles. But few realize that the Will may be developed and strengthened by intelligent practice. They feel that they could accomplish wonders if they had a strong Will, but instead of attempting to develop it, they content themselves with vain regrets. They sigh, but do nothing.

Those who have investigated the subject closely know that Will Power, with all its latent possibilities and mighty powers, may be developed, disciplined, controlled and directed, just as may be any other of Nature's forces. It does not matter what theory you may entertain about the nature of the Will, you will obtain the results if you practice intelligently.

Personally, I have a somewhat odd theory about the Will. I believe that every man has, potentially, a strong Will, and that all he has to do is to train his mind to make use of it. I think that in the higher regions of the mind of every man is a great store of Will Power awaiting his use, and the supply is unlimited, for your little storage battery is connected with the great power house of the Universal Will Power, and the power is inexhaustible.

Your Will does not need training, but your Mind does. The mind is the instrument and the supply of Will Power is proportionate to the fitness of the instrument through which it manifests. But you needn't accept this theory if you don't like it. This lesson will fit your theory as well as mine.

A man who has developed his mind so that it will allow the Will Power to manifest through it, has opened up wonderful possibilities for himself. Not only has he found a great power at his command, but he is able to bring into play, and use, faculties, talents and abilities of whose existence he has not dreamed. This secret of the Will is the magic key which opens all doors.

The late Donald G. Mitchell once wrote:

"Resolve is what makes a man manifest; not puny resolve, but crude determination; not errant purpose - but that strong and indefatigable will which treads down difficulties and danger, as a boy treads down the heaving frost-lands of winter; which kindles his eye and brain with a proud pulse-beat toward the unattainable. Will makes men giants."

Many of us feel that if we would but exert our Will, we might accomplish wonders. But somehow we do not seem to want to take the trouble. We put it off from time to time, and talk vaguely of "some day," but that some day never comes.

We instinctively feel the power of the Will, but we haven't enough energy to exercise it, and so drift along with the tide, unless perhaps some friendly difficulty arises, some helpful obstacle appears in our path, or some kindly pain stirs us into action, in either of which cases we are compelled to assert our Will and thus begin to accomplish something.

The trouble with us is that we do not want to do the thing enough to make us exert our

Will Power. We don't want it hard enough. We are mentally lazy and of weak resolve. That is the trouble. Let a man be in danger of losing his life - let a woman be in danger of losing a great love - and you will witness a startling exhibition of Will Power from an unexpected source. Let a woman's child be threatened with danger, and she will manifest a degree of Courage and Will that sweeps all before it, and yet the same woman will quail before a domineering husband, and will lack the Will to perform a simple task.

Strong will follows strong desire

A boy will do all sorts of work if he but considers it play, and yet he can scarcely force himself to cut a little firewood. Strong Will follows strong Desire. If you really want to do a thing very much, you can usually develop the Will Power to accomplish it.

The trouble is that you have not really wanted to do these things, and yet you blame your Will. You say that you do want to do it, but if you stop to think you will see that you really want to do something else more than the thing in question. You are not willing to pay the price of attainment. Stop a moment and analyze this statement and apply it to your own case.

You are mentally lazy - that's the trouble. Don't talk to me about not having enough Will. You have a great storehouse of Will awaiting your use, but you are too lazy to use it. Now, if you are really in earnest about this matter, get to work and first find out what you really want to do - then start to work and do it. Never mind about the Will Power, you'll find a full supply of that whenever you need it. The thing to do is to get to the point where you will resolve to do something. That's the real test - the resolving. Think of these things a little, and make up your mind whether or not you really want something sufficiently hard to get to work.

There are many exercises designed to "strengthen" the Will, but what these exercises really do is strengthen the Mind so that it is able to draw upon its store of power.

AUTO-SUGGESTION:

I Am Using My Will Power

Say these words several times earnestly and positively, immediately after finishing this article. Then repeat them frequently during the day, at least once an hour, and particularly when you meet something that calls for the exercise of Will Power.

Also repeat them several times after you retire and settle yourself for sleep. Now, there is nothing in these words unless you back them up with the thought. In fact, the thought is everything, and the words only pegs upon which to hang the thought. So think of what you are saying, and mean what you say. You must use Faith at the start, and use the words with a confident expectation of the result. Hold the steady thought that you are drawing on your storehouse of Will Power, and before long you will find that thought is taking form in action, and that your Will Power is manifesting itself. You will feel an influx of strength with each repetition of the words. You will find yourself overcoming difficulties and bad habits, and will be surprised at how things are being smoothed out for you.

EXERCISE:

Perform at least one disagreeable task each day during the month.

If there is any especially disagreeable task which you would like to shirk, that is the one for you to perform. This exercise is not given to you in order to make you self-sacrificing or meek, or anything of that sort, it is given to you to exercise your Will. Anyone can do a pleasant thing cheerfully, but it takes Will to do the unpleasant thing cheerfully; and that is how you must do the work. It will prove a most valuable discipline to you. Try it for a month and you will see an amazing change in yourself, and in what you accomplish.

If you shirk this exercise you had better stop right here and acknowledge that you do not want Will Power, and are content to stay where you are and remain a weakling.

Chapter 5 Summary

• Will power can be developed with practice

• We always do what we really want to do

• Anyone can do a pleasant thing cheerfully, but it takes Will to do unpleasant things cheerfully

"I have known a great many troubles, but most of them never happened."

Mark Twain

Become Immune to Damaging Thoughts 6

Fear is a habit

To become immune to damaging thoughts the first thing you must do is cut out Fear and Worry. Fear thoughts are the cause of much unhappiness and many failures. You have been told this thing over and over again, but it will bear repeating. Fear is a habit of mind from which we may free ourselves by individual effort and perseverance.

Strong expectancy is a powerful magnet. A person of strong, confident desire attracts the things best calculated to aid him - persons, things, circumstances, surroundings; if he desires them hopefully, trustfully, confidently, and calmly. Equally true, he who Fears a thing generally manages to start into operation forces which will cause the thing he feared to come upon him. Don't you see, the man who Fears really expects the feared thing, and in the eyes of the Law it is the same as if he really had wished for or desired it? The Law is operative in both cases - the principle is the same.

Courage

The best way to overcome the habit of Fear is to assume the mental attitude of Courage, just as the best way to get rid of darkness is to let in the light. It is a waste of time to fight a negative thought-habit by recognizing its force and trying to deny it out of existence by mighty efforts. The best, surest, easiest and quickest method is to assume the existence of the positive thought desired in its place; and by constantly dwelling upon the positive thought, manifest it into objective reality.

Therefore, instead of repeating, "I'm not afraid," say boldly, "I am full of Courage," "I am Courageous." You must assert, "There's nothing to fear," which, although in the nature of a denial, simply denies the reality of the object causing fear rather than admitting the fear itself and then denying it.

To overcome Fear, one should hold firmly to the mental attitude of Courage. He should think Courage, say Courage, act Courage. He should keep the mental picture of Courage before him all the time, until it becomes his normal mental attitude. Hold the ideal firmly before you and you will gradually grow to its attainment - the ideal will become manifest.

Let the word "Courage" sink deeply into your mind, and then hold it firmly there until the mind fastens it in place. Think of yourself as being Courageous - see yourself as acting with Courage in trying situations. Realize that there is nothing to Fear, that Worry and Fear never helped anyone, and never will. Realize that Fear paralyzes effort, and that Courage promotes activity.

"I Can and I Will"

The confident, fearless, expectant, "I Can and I Will" man is a mighty magnet. He attracts to himself just what is needed for his success. Things seem to come his way, and people say he is "lucky." Nonsense! "Luck" has nothing to do with it. It's all in the Mental Attitude.

The Mental Attitude of the "I Can't" or the "I'm Afraid" man also determines his measure of success. There's no mystery whatsoever about it. You have but to look about you to realize the truth of what I have said. Did you ever know a successful man who did not have the "I Can and I Will" thought strong within him? Why, he will walk all around the "I Can't" man, who has perhaps even more ability.

The first mental attitude brought to the surface latent qualities, as well as attracted help from outside; whilst the second mental attitude not only attracted "I Can't" people and things, but also kept the man's own powers from manifesting themselves.

Use your thoughts to your advantage

Don't waste your Thought-Force, but use it to advantage. Stop attracting to yourself failure, unhappiness, disharmony, and sorrow. Begin now and send out a current of bright, positive, happy thought. Let your prevailing thought be "I Can and I Will;" think "I Can and I Will;" dream "I Can and I Will;" say "I Can and I Will;" act "I Can and I Will." Live on the "I Can and I Will" plane. Before long you will feel the new vibrations manifesting themselves in action; will see them bring results; will be conscious of the new point of view; and will realize that your own is coming to you. You will feel better, act better, see better, BE better in every way, after you join the "I Can and I Will" brigade.

Fear is the parent, of Worry, Hate, Jealousy, Malice, Anger, Discontent, Failure and all the rest. The man who rids himself of Fear will find that the rest of the brood have disappeared. The only way to be Free is to get rid of Fear. Tear it out by the roots. I regard the conquest of Fear as the first important step to be taken by those who wish to master the application of Thought Force. So long as Fear masters you, you are in no condition to make progress in the realm of Thought, so start to work at once to get rid of this obstruction. You CAN do it - if you only go about it in earnest. When you have ridded yourself of the vile thing, life will seem entirely different to you - you will feel happier, freer, stronger, more positive, and will be more successful in every undertaking of Life.

Start today, make up your mind that this intruder must GO. Do not compromise matters with him, but insist upon an absolute surrender on his part. You will find the task difficult at first, but each time you oppose him he will grow weaker, and you will be stronger. Shut off his nourishment - starve him to death - he cannot live in a thought-atmosphere of Fearlessness. So, start to fill your mind with good, strong, Fearless thoughts. Keep yourself busy thinking Fearlessness, and Fear will die of his own accord. Fearlessness is positive - Fear is negative, and you may be sure that the positive will prevail.

So long as Fear is around with his "but," "if," "suppose," "I'm afraid," "I can't," "what if," and all the rest of his cowardly suggestions, you will not be able to use your Thought Force to the best advantage. Once you get him out of the way, you will have clear sailing, and every inch of thought-sail will catch the wind. He is a Jonah. Overboard with him! (The whale that swallows him will have my sympathy.)

Start in to do some of the things which you feel you could do if you were not afraid to try. Start to work to do these things, affirming "Courage" all the way through, and you will be surprised to see how the changed mental attitude will clear away obstacles from your path, and will make things much easier than you had anticipated. Exercises of this kind will develop you wonderfully, and you will be much gratified at the result of a little practice along these lines.

There are many things before you that you can accomplish if you will only throw aside the yoke of Fear - if you will boldly assert the "I" and its power. The best way to vanquish Fear is to assert "Courage" and stop thinking of Fear. Train the mind into new habits of thought, thus eradicating the old negative thoughts which have been pulling you down, and holding you back. Take the word "Courage" with you as your watchword and manifest it in action.

Remember, the only thing to fear is Fear, and - well, don't even fear Fear, for he's a cowardly chap at the best, who will run if you show a brave front.

Chapter 6 Summary

• Become immune to damaging thoughts by cutting out Fear and Worry

• Strong expectancy is a powerful magnet

• The mental attitude of **"I Can"** creates success

• The mental attitude of **"I'm afraid"** creates failure

"You can never become a great man or woman until you have overcome anxiety, worry, and fear.

It is impossible for an anxious person, a worried one, or a fearful one to perceive truth; all things are distorted and thrown out of their proper relations by such mental states, ..."

Wallace D. Wattles

7

Transforming Negative Thoughts

Worry stands in the way of accomplishment

Worry is the child of Fear. If you kill off Fear, Worry will die for want of nourishment. This is very old advice, and yet it is always worthy of repetition, for it is a lesson of which we are greatly in need.

Some people think that if we kill out Fear and Worry we will never be able to accomplish anything. I have read editorials in the great journals in which the writers held that without Worry one can never accomplish any of the great tasks of life, because Worry is necessary to stimulate interest and work. This is nonsense, no matter who utters it.

Worry never helped one to accomplish anything; on the contrary, it stands in the way of accomplishment and attainment.

Desire and Interest

The motive underlying action and "doing things" is Desire and Interest. If one earnestly desires a thing, he naturally becomes very much interested in its accomplishment, and is quick to seize upon anything likely to help him to gain the thing he wants. More than that, his mind starts to work on the subconscious plane to bring into the field of consciousness many ideas of value and importance. Desire and Interest are the causes that result in success.

Worry is not Desire. It is true that if one's surroundings and environments become intolerable, he is driven in desperation to some efforts that will result in throwing off the undesirable conditions and in the acquiring of those more in harmony with his desire. But this is really only another form of Desire - the man desires something different from what he has; and when his desire becomes strong enough his entire interest is given to the task, he makes a mighty effort, and the change is accomplished. But it wasn't Worry that caused the effort. Worry could content itself with wringing its hands and moaning "Woe is me," and wearing its nerves to a frazzle, and accomplishing nothing.

Desire acts differently. It grows stronger as the man's conditions become intolerable, and finally when he feels the hurt so strongly that he can't stand it any longer, he says, "I won't stand this any longer, I will make a change," and then Desire springs into action. The man keeps on "wanting" a change and his Interest and Attention being given to the task of deliverance, he begins to make things move.

Worry never accomplished anything. Worry is negative and death producing. Desire and Ambition are positive and life producing. A man may worry himself to death and yet nothing will be accomplished, but let that man transmute his worry and discontent into Desire and Interest, coupled with a belief that he is able to make the change - the "I Can and I Will" idea - then something happens.

Yes, Fear and Worry must go before we can do much. One must proceed to cast out these negative intruders, and replace them with Confidence and Hope. Transform Worry into keen Desire. Then you will find that Interest is awakened, and you will begin to think things of interest to you. Thoughts will come to you from the great reserve stock in your mind and you will start to manifest them in action. Moreover you will be placing yourself in harmony with similar thoughts of others, and will draw to you aid and assistance from the great volume of thought waves with which the world is filled. Man draws to himself thought waves corresponding in character with the nature of the prevailing thoughts in his own mind - his mental attitude. Then again, he begins to set into motion the great Law of Attraction, whereby he draws to him others likely to help him, and is, in turn, attracted to others who can aid him. This Law of Attraction is no joke, no metaphysical absurdity, but is a great live working principle of Nature, as anyone may learn by experimenting and observing.

Are you willing to pay the price?

To succeed in anything you must want it very much. Desire must be in evidence in order to attract. The man of weak desires attracts very little to himself. The stronger the desire the greater the force set into motion. You must want a thing hard enough before you can get it. You must want it more than you do the things around you, and you must be prepared to pay the price for it. The price is the throwing overboard of certain lesser desires that stand in the way of the accomplishment of the greater one. Comfort, ease, leisure, amusements, and many other things may have to go (not always, though). It all depends on what you want.

As a rule, the greater the thing desired, the greater the price to be paid for it. Nature believes in adequate compensation. But if you really Desire a thing in earnest, you will pay the price without question; for the Desire will dwarf the importance of the other things.

You say that you want a thing very much, and are doing everything possible toward its attainment? No, you are only playing Desire. Do you want the thing as much as a prisoner wants freedom? As much as a dying man wants life? Look at the almost miraculous things accomplished by prisoners desiring freedom. Look how they work through steel plates and stone walls with a bit of stone. Is your desire as strong as that? Do you work for the desired thing as if your life depended upon it? Nonsense, you don't know what Desire is. If a man wants a thing as much as the prisoner wants freedom, or as much as a strongly vital man wants life, then that man will be able to sweep away obstacles and impediments apparently immovable. The key to attainment is Desire, Confidence, and Will. This key will open many doors.

Fear paralyzes Desire

Fear paralyzes Desire - it scares the life out of it. You must get rid of Fear. There have been times in my life when Fear would get hold of me and take a good, firm grip on my vitals, and I would lose all hope; all interest; all ambition; all desire. But fortunately, I have always managed to throw off the grip of the monster and face my difficulty like a man; and things would always be straightened out for me somehow. Either the difficulty would melt away, or I would be given means to overcome it, or get around, or under or over it. It is strange how this works. No matter how great the difficulty, when we finally face it with courage and confidence in ourselves, we seem to pull through somehow, and then we begin to wonder what we were scared about. This is not a mere fancy, it is the working of a mighty law, which we do not yet fully understand, but which proves itself every time.

People often say: "It's all very well for you New Thought people to say don't worry, but what's a person to do when he thinks of all the possible things ahead of him, which might upset him and his plans?"

Well, all that I can say is that the man is foolish to bother about thinking of troubles to come at some time in the future. The majority of things that we worry about never come to pass at all; a large proportion of the others come in a milder form than we had anticipated, and there are always other things which come at the same time which help us to overcome the trouble. The future holds in store for us not only difficulties to be overcome, but also agents to help us in overcoming the difficulties. Things adjust themselves. We are prepared for any trouble which may come upon us, and when the time comes we somehow find ourselves able to meet it.

90% of worries never come to pass

It has been said that nine-tenths of our worries are over things which never come to pass, and that the other tenth is over things of little or no account. So what's the use in using up all your reserve force in fretting over future troubles, if this be so? Better wait until your troubles really come before you worry. You will find that by this storing up of energy you will be able to meet any sort of trouble that comes your way.

What is it that uses up all the energy in the average man or woman, anyway? Is it the real overcoming of difficulties, or the worrying about impending troubles? It's always "Tomorrow, tomorrow," and yet tomorrow never comes just as we feared it would. Tomorrow is all right; it carries in its grip good things as well as troubles. Bless my soul, when I sit down and think over the things which I once feared might possibly descend upon me, I laugh! Where are those feared things now? I don't know, I have almost forgotten that I ever feared them.

You do not need to fight Worry - that isn't the way to overcome the habit. Just practice concentration, and then learn to concentrate upon something right before you, and you will find that the worry thought has vanished.

The mind can think of but one thing at a time, and if you concentrate upon a bright thing, the other thing will fade away. There are better ways of overcoming objectionable thoughts than by fighting them. Learn to concentrate upon thoughts of an opposite character, and you will have solved the problem.

When the mind is full of worry thoughts, it cannot find time to work out plans to benefit you. But when you have concentrated upon bright, helpful thoughts, you will discover that it will start to work subconsciously; and when the time comes you will find all sorts of plans and methods by which you will be able to meet the demands upon you. Keep your mental attitude right, and all things will be added unto you. There's no sense in worrying; nothing has ever been gained by it, and nothing ever will be. Bright, cheerful and happy thoughts attract bright, cheerful and happy things to us - worry drives them away. Cultivate the right mental attitude.

Chapter 7 Summary

- Worry stands in the way of accomplishment

- Desire and Interest are the motives underlying action

- To succeed in anything you must want it very much

- If you really Desire something you will be willing to pay the price

- When you face your fears with courage and confidence you will pull through somehow, and then wonder what you were scared about

- You can only think about one thing at a time, if you concentrate upon a positive thing, the negative things will fade away

"Concentrate all your thoughts upon the work at hand. The sun's rays do not burn until brought to a focus."

Alexander Graham Bell

The Law of Mental Control

8

Control your thoughts or they will control you

Your thoughts are either faithful servants or tyrannical masters - whichever you allow them to be. You have the say about it; take your choice. They will either go about your work under direction of the firm will, doing it the best they know how, or they will ride all over us and make us their slaves if we are foolish enough to allow them to do so. More than half the people of the world are slaves of every vagrant thought which may see fit to torment them.

Your thoughts go about their work not only in your waking hours, but also when you are asleep. Some of our best mental work being performed for us when our conscious mentality is at rest, as is evidenced by the fact that when the morning comes we find troublesome problems have been worked out for us during the night, after we had apparently dismissed them from our minds.

Your mind is given you for your good and for your own use, not to use you. There are very few people who seem to realize this and who understand the art of managing the mind. The key to the mystery is Concentration. A little practice will develop within every man the power to use the mental machine properly. When you have some mental work to do concentrate upon it to the exclusion of everything else, and you will find that the mind will get right down to business - to the work at hand - and matters will be cleared up in no time. There is an absence of friction, and all waste motion or lost power is avoided. Every pound of energy is put to use, and every revolution of the mental driving-wheel counts for something.

The man who understands how to run his mental engine knows that one of the most important things is to be able to stop it when the work has been done. He does not keep putting coal in the furnace, and maintaining a high pressure after the work is finished, or when the day's portion of the work has been done, and the fires should be banked until the next day. Some people act as if the engine should be kept running whether there was any work to be done or not, and then they complain if it gets worn out and wobbles and needs repairing. These mental engines are fine machines, and need intelligent care.

Focus your mind and get a good night's sleep

To those who are acquainted with the laws of mental control it seems absurd for one to lie awake at night fretting about the problems of the day, or more often, of the morrow. It is just as easy to slow down the mind as it is to slow down an engine. The best way to do it is to think of something else - as far different from the obtruding thought as possible. There is no use fighting an objectionable thought; that is a great waste of energy, and the more you keep on saying, "I won't think of this thing!" the more it keeps on coming into your mind, for you are holding it there for the purpose of hitting it. Let it go; don't give it another thought; fix the mind on something entirely different, and keep the attention there by an effort of the will. A little practice will do much for you in this direction.

There is only room for one thing at a time in the focus of attention; so put all your attention upon one thought, and the others will sneak off. Try it for yourself.

Chapter 8 Summary

• Your thoughts are either faithful servants or tyrannical masters

• Our minds are working even when we are asleep

• There is no use in fighting a negative thought, simply put your attention on something else and the negative thought will disappear

9

Start to Really Live

Put some life into your life

I have spoken to you of the advantage of getting rid of Fear. Now I wish to put LIFE into you.

Many of you have been going along as if you were dead - no ambition - no energy - no vitality - no interest. This will never do. You are stagnating. Wake up and display a few signs of life! This is not the place in which you can stalk around like a living corpse - this is the place for wide-awake, active, live people, and a good general awakening is what is needed; although it would take nothing less than a blast from Gabriel's trumpet to awaken some of the people who are stalking around thinking that they are alive, but who are really dead to all that makes life worth while.

We must let Life flow through us, and allow it to express itself naturally. Do not let the little worries

65

of life, or the big ones either, depress you and cause you to lose your vitality. Assert the Life Force within you, and manifest it in every thought, act and deed, and before long you will be exhilarated and fairly bubbling over with vitality and energy.

Take an active interest in what you are doing

Put a little life into your work - into your pleasures - into yourself. Stop doing things in a half-hearted way, and begin to take an interest in what you are doing, saying and thinking. It is astonishing how much interest we may find in the ordinary things of life, if we will only wake up. There are interesting things all around us - interesting events occurring every moment - but we will not be aware of them unless we assert our life force and begin to actually live instead of merely existing.

No man or woman ever amounted to anything unless he or she put life into the tasks of everyday life - the acts - the thoughts. What the world needs is live men and women. Just look into the eyes of the people whom you meet, and see how few of them are really alive. The most of them lack that expression of conscious life which distinguishes the man who lives from the one who simply exists.

Acquire this sense of conscious life so that you may manifest it in your life.

AFFIRMATION & EXERCISE:

"I Am Alive."

Fix in your mind the thought that the "I" within you is very much alive and that you are manifesting life fully, mentally and physically. Keep this thought there, aiding yourself with constant repetitions of the watchword. Don't let the thought escape you, but keep pushing it back into the mind. Keep it before the mental vision as much as possible. Repeat the watchword when you awaken in the morning - say it when you retire at night. Say it at meal times, and whenever else you can during the day - at least once an hour.

Form the mental picture of yourself as filled with Life and Energy. Live up to it as far as possible. When you start in to perform a task say "I Am Alive" and mix up as much life as possible in the task. If you find yourself feeling depressed, say "I Am Alive," and then take a few deep breaths, and with each inhalation let the mind hold the thought that you are breathing in Strength and Life, and as you exhale, hold the thought that you are breathing out all the old, dead, negative conditions and are glad to get rid of them.

Finish up with an earnest, vigorous affirmation: "I Am Alive," and mean it when you say it.

Let your thoughts take form in action. Don't rest content with merely saying that you are alive, but prove it with your actions. Take an interest in doing things, and don't go around "mooning" or day-dreaming. Get down to business, and LIVE.

Are you bored with your life?

If your life doesn't excite you it is time for you to make some changes. Often we get into ruts and just keep going along doing the same thing over and over again long after it ceases to interest us.

Life is too short to spend it just going along waiting for something far off in the future that may never come. So many people stay in unhappy marriages thinking that they don't have choices. Other people go to jobs they hate waiting for retirement so that they can start to live, only to find out that by then their health or their finances won't allow them to enjoy life.

Live your life NOW, the future doesn't come with any guarantees!

Chapter 9 Summary

- Put some life into your life

- Don't let the worries of life depress you

- Take an interest in what you are doing

- Breathe deeply

- Live life NOW

"Excellence is not a singular act, but a habit. You are what you repeatedly do."

Shaquille O'Neal

Forming Habits

10

Develop some useful new habits

Professor William James, a well-known teacher of Psychology, says:

> "The great thing in all education is to make our nervous system our ally instead of our enemy. For this we must make automatic and habitual, as early as possible, as many useful actions as we can, and as carefully guard against growing into ways that are likely to be disadvantageous. In the acquisition of a new habit, or the leaving off of an old one, we must take care to launch ourselves with as strong and decided initiative as possible. Never suffer an exception to occur until the new habit is securely rooted in your life. Seize the very first possible opportunity to act on every resolution you make and on every emotional prompting you may experience, in the direction of the habits you aspire to gain."

Habits are easy to make and hard to break

This advice is familiar to all students of New Thought, but it states the matter more plainly than the majority of us have done. It impresses upon us the importance of passing on to the subconscious mind the proper impulses, so that they will become automatic and "second nature."

Our subconscious mind is a great store house for all sorts of suggestions from ourselves and others, and, as it is the "habit-mind," we must be careful to send it the proper material from which it may make habits. If we get into the habit of doing certain things, we may be sure that the subconscious mind will make it easier for us to do just the same thing over and over again, easier each time, until finally we are firmly bound with the ropes and chains of the habit, and find it more or less difficult, sometimes almost impossible, to free ourselves from the hateful thing.

We should cultivate good habits against the hour of need. The time will come when we will be required to put forth our best efforts, and it rests with us today whether that hour of need shall find us doing the proper thing automatically and almost without thought, or struggling to do it bound down and hindered with the chains of things opposed to that which we desire at that moment.

We must be on guard at all times to prevent the forming of undesirable habits. There may be no special harm in doing a certain thing today, or perhaps even again tomorrow, but there may be much harm in setting up the habit of doing that particular thing on into the future. If you are confronted with the question: "Which of these two things should I do?" the best answer is: "I will do that which I would like to become a habit with me."

In forming a new habit, or in breaking an old one, we should throw ourselves into the task with as much enthusiasm as possible, in order to gain the most ground before the energy expends itself when it meets with friction from the opposing habits already formed. We should start in by making as strong an impression as possible upon the subconscious mentality. Then we should be constantly on guard against temptations to break the new resolution "just this once." This "just once" idea kills off more good resolutions than any other one cause. The moment you yield "just this once," you introduce the thin edge of the wedge that will, in the end, split your resolution into pieces.

Equally important is the fact that each time you resist temptation the stronger does your resolution become. Act upon your resolution as early and as often as possible, as with every manifestation of thought in action, the stronger does it become. You are adding to the strength of your original resolution every time you back it up with action.

Folds in a piece of paper

The mind has been likened to a piece of paper that has been folded. Ever afterwards it has a tendency to fold in the same crease unless we make a new crease or fold. The creases are habits, every time we make one it is so much easier for the mind to fold along the same crease afterward. Let us make our mental creases in the right direction.

Chapter 10 Summary

• Habits are easy to make and hard to break so cultivate good habits

• Each time you resist temptation your resolve grows stronger

---

The Psychology of Emotion

11

Emotions are habits

We often think of emotions as independent from habit. We easily think of one acquiring habits of action, and even of thinking, but we are apt to regard the emotions as something connected with "feeling" and quite divorced from intellectual effort. Yet both are dependent largely upon habit, and one may repress, increase, develop, and change one's emotions, just as one may regulate habits of action and lines of thought.

We know that emotions deepen by repetition. If a person allows a state of feeling to thoroughly take possession of him, he will find it easier to yield to the same emotion the second time, and so on, until the particular emotion or feeling becomes second nature to him.

If an undesirable emotion shows itself inclined

to take up a permanent abode with you, you had better start to work to get rid of it, or at least to master it. The best time to do this is at the start; for each repetition renders the habit more firmly entrenched, and the task of dislodging it more difficult.

Were you ever jealous? If so, you will remember how insidious was its first approach, how subtly it whispered hateful suggestions into your willing ear, and how gradually it followed up such suggestions, until, finally you began to see green. Then you will remember how the thing seemed to grow, taking possession of you until you scarcely could shake it off. You found it much easier to become jealous the next time. It seemed to bring before you all sorts of objects apparently justifying your suspicions. Everything began to look green.

Emotions grow each time we express them

So it is with every feeling or emotion. If you give way to a fit of rage, you will find it easier to become angry the next time, on less provocation. The habit of feeling and acting "mean" does not take long to firmly settle itself in its new home if encouraged.

Worry is a great habit for growing. People start by worrying about big things, then begin to worry and fret about some smaller thing, and then the merest trifle worries and distresses them. They imagine that all sorts of evil things are about to befall them. If they start on a journey they are certain there is going to be a wreck. If a telegram comes, it is sure to contain some dreadful tidings. If a child seems a little quiet, the worrying mother is positive it is going to fall ill and die. If the husband seems thoughtful, as he revolves some business plan in his mind, then the good wife is convinced that he is beginning to cease to love her, and indulges in a crying spell. And so it goes - worry, worry, worry - each indulgence making the habit more at home. After a while the continued thought shows itself in action. Not only is the mind poisoned by the blue thoughts, but the forehead shows deep lines between the eyebrows, and the voice takes on that whining, rasping tone so common among worry-burdened people.

The condition of mind known as "fault-finding" is another emotion that grows fat with exercise. First, fault is found with this thing, then with that, and finally with everything. The person becomes a chronic "nagger"- a burden to friends and relatives, and a thing to be avoided by outsiders. This nagging is all a matter of habit. It grows from small beginnings, and each time it is indulged in it throws out another root, branch, or tendril, and fastens itself the closer to the one who has given it soil in which to grow.

Envy, uncharitableness, gossip, scandal-mongering, are all habits of this kind. The seeds are in every human being, and only need good soil and a little watering to become lusty and strong.

Each time you give way to one of these negative emotions, the easier do you make it for a recurrence of the same thing, or similar ones. Sometimes by encouraging one unworthy emotion, you find that you have given room for the growth of a whole family of these mental weeds.

I am not endeavoring to be like a Bible preacher, railing against the sin of bad thoughts. I am merely calling your attention to the law underlying the psychology of emotions. There is nothing new about this, it is as old as the hills, so old that many of us have forgotten all about it.

If you wish to manifest these constantly disagreeable and unpleasant traits, and to suffer the unhappiness that comes from them, by all means do so, that is your own business, and privilege. It's none of mine, and I am kept busy enough minding my own business and keeping an eye on my own undesirable habits and actions. I am merely telling you the law regarding the matter, and you may do the rest.

Repress and choke out negative emotions

If you wish to choke out these habits, there are two ways open to you. First, whenever you find yourself indulging in a negative thought or feeling, take right hold of it and say to it firmly, and vigorously, "Get out!" It won't like this at first, and will bridle up, curve its back and snarl like an offended cat. But never mind, just say "Scat" to it. The next time it will not be so confident and aggressive, it will have manifested a little of the fear-habit. Each time you repress and choke out a tendency of this kind, the weaker it will become, and the stronger will your will be.

Professor James says:

"Refuse to express a passion, and it dies. Count ten before venting your anger, and its occasion seems ridiculous. Whistling to keep up courage is no mere figure of speech. On the other hand, sit all day in a moping posture, sigh, and reply to everything with a dismal voice, and your melancholy lingers. There is no more valuable precept in moral education than this, as all who have experience know: if we wish to conquer emotional tendencies in ourselves, we must assiduously, and in the first instance, cold-bloodedly, go through the outward movements of those contrary dispositions which we prefer

to cultivate. Smooth the brow, brighten the eye, contract the dorsal rather than the ventral aspect of the frame, and speak in a major key, pass the genial compliment, and your heart must be frigid indeed if it does not gradually thaw."

Chapter 11 Summary

• Emotions are a habit

• Emotions grow each time we express them

• Repress and choke out negative emotions by refusing to express them

---

Developing New Thought Patterns 12

Cultivate positive emotions

I have spoken of the plan of getting rid of undesirable states of feeling by driving them out. But a far better way is to cultivate the feeling or emotion directly opposed to the one you wish to eradicate.

We are very apt to regard ourselves as the creatures of our emotions and feelings, and to fancy that these feelings and emotions are "we." But such is far from being the truth. It is true that most people are the slaves of their emotions and feelings, and are governed by them to a great degree. They think that feelings are things that rule one and from which one cannot free himself, and so they cease to rebel. They yield to the feeling without question, although they may know that the emotion or mental trait is calculated to injure them, and to bring unhappiness and failure instead of happiness and success. They say "we are made that way," and let it go at that.

The new Psychology is teaching people better things. It tells them that they are masters of their emotions and feelings, instead of being their slaves. It tells them that thought patterns may be developed that will manifest along desirable lines, and that the old thought patterns that have been manifesting so unpleasantly may be placed on the retired list, and allowed to atrophy from want of use.

People can make themselves over, and change their entire natures. This is not mere idle theory, but is a working fact which has been demonstrated by thousands of people.

The brain is the instrument of the mind

No matter what theory of mind we adhere to, we must admit that the brain is the organ and instrument of the mind, in our present state of existence, at least, and that the brain must be considered in this matter. The brain is like a wonderful musical instrument, having millions of keys, upon which we may play innumerable combinations of sounds.

We come into the world with certain tendencies, temperaments, and predispositions. We may account for these tendencies by heredity, or we may account for them upon theories of pre-existence, but the facts remain the same. Certain keys seem to respond to our touch more easily than others. Certain notes seem to sound forth as the current of circumstances sweeps over the strings. While certain other notes are less easily vibrated. But we find that if we but make an effort of the will to restrain the utterance of some of these easily sounded strings, they will grow more difficult to sound, and less liable to be stirred by the passing breeze. If we will pay attention to some of the other strings that have not been giving forth a clear tone, we will soon get them in good working order; their notes will chime forth clear and vibrant, and will drown the less pleasant sounds.

We have millions of unused brain-cells awaiting our cultivation. We are using but a few of them, and some of these we are working to death. We are able to give some of these cells a rest, by using other cells. The brain may be trained and cultivated in a manner incredible to one who has not looked into the subject. Mental attitudes may be acquired and cultivated, changed and discarded, at will.

There is no longer any excuse for people manifesting unpleasant and harmful mental states. We have the remedy in our own hands.

We are creatures of habit

We acquire habits of thought, feeling, and action, by repeated use. We may be born with a tendency in a certain direction, or we may acquire tendencies by suggestions from others; such as the examples of those around us, suggestions from reading, listening to teachers. We are a bundle of mental habits. Each time we indulge in an undesirable thought or habit, the easier does it become to repeat that thought or action. The more often we give forth a certain desirable thought, or perform a desirable action, the easier does it become for us to repeat that thought or action.

Mental scientists are in the habit of speaking of desirable thoughts or mental attitudes as "positive," and of the undesirable ones as "negative." There is a good reason for this. The mind instinctively recognizes certain things as good for the individual to which it belongs, and it clears the path for such thoughts, and interposes the least resistance to them. They have a much greater effect than an undesirable thought possesses, and one positive thought will counteract a number of negative thoughts. The best way to overcome undesirable or negative thoughts and feelings is to cultivate the positive ones. The positive thought is the strongest plant, and will in time starve out the negative one by withdrawing from it the nourishment necessary for its existence.

Weeds of the mind

Of course the negative thought will set up a vigorous resistance at first, for it is a fight for life with it. It knows it is finished if the positive thought is allowed to grow and develop; and, consequently, it makes things unpleasant for the individual until he has started well into the work of starving it out. Brain cells do not like to be laid on the shelf any more than does any other form of living energy, and they rebel and struggle until they become too weak to do so. The best way is to pay as little attention as possible to these weeds of the mind, but put in as much time as possible watering, caring for and attending to the new and beautiful plants in the garden of the mind.

Act the way you want to become

For instance, if you are apt to hate people, you can best overcome the negative thought by cultivating Love in its place. Think Love, and act it out, as often as possible. Cultivate thoughts of kindness, and act as kindly as you can to everyone with whom you come in contact. You will have trouble at the start, but gradually Love will master Hate, and the latter will begin to droop and wither.

If you have a tendency toward the "blues" cultivate a smile, and a cheerful view of things. Insist upon your mouth wearing upturned corners, and make an effort of the will to look upon the bright side of things. The "blue-devils" will set up a fight, of course, but pay no attention to them, just go on cultivating optimism and cheerfulness. Let "Bright, Cheerful and Happy" be your mantra, and try to live it out.

These ideas may seem very old and time worn, but they are psychological truths and may be used by you to advantage. If you once comprehend the nature of the thing, the affirmations and auto-suggestions of the several schools may be understood and taken advantage of. You may make yourself energetic instead of slothful, active instead of lazy, by this method. It is all a matter of practice and steady work.

Thoughts take action; actions influence thoughts

New Thought people often have much to say about "holding the thought;" and, indeed, it is necessary to "hold the thought" in order to accomplish results. But something more is needed. You must "act out" the thought until it becomes a fixed habit with you. Thoughts take form in action; and in turn actions influence thought. So by "acting out" certain lines of thought, the actions react upon the mind, and increase the development of the part of the mind having close relation to the act. Each time the mind entertains a thought, the easier becomes the resulting action, and each time an act is performed, the easier becomes the corresponding thought. So you see the thing works both ways - action and reaction. If you feel cheerful and happy, it is very natural for you to laugh. And if you will laugh a little, you will begin to feel bright and cheerful.

Do you see what I am trying to get at? Here it is, in a nutshell: you wish to cultivate a certain habit of action, begin by cultivating the mental attitude corresponding to it. As a means of cultivating that mental attitude, start in to "act-out," or go through, the motions of the act corresponding to the thought. Now, see if you cannot apply this rule. Take up something that you really feel should be done, but which you do not feel like doing. Cultivate the thought leading up to it, say to yourself: "I like to do so and so," and then go through the motions (cheerfully, remember!) and act out the thought that you like to do the thing. Take an interest in the doing- study out the best way to do it - put brains into it-take a pride in it - and you will find yourself doing the thing with a considerable amount of pleasure and interest. You will have cultivated a new habit.

I Can and I Will

If you prefer trying it on some mental trait of which you wish to be rid, it will work the same way. Start in to cultivate the opposite trait, and think it out and act it out for all you are worth. Then watch the change that will come over you. Don't be discouraged at the resistance you will encounter at first, but sing gaily: *"I Can and I Will,"* and get to work in earnest. The important thing in this work is to keep cheerful and interested. If you manage to do this, the rest will be easy.

Chapter 12 Summary

• We are creatures of habit

• Each time we indulge in a thought or habit, the easier it is to repeat

• The brain is the instrument of the mind

• We are born with certain tendencies, and we acquire tendencies from others

• Attitudes may be acquired and cultivated, changed and discarded, at will

• Act the way you want to become

• Thoughts take form in action; and actions influence thoughts

• Remember, *"I Can and I Will"*

*"Choose a job you love,
and you will never have to work
a day in your life."*

Confucius

The Focusing Power of Love

13

Concentrate your mental force

We have discussed the necessity of getting rid of fear, that your desire may have full strength with which to work. Supposing that you have mastered this part of the task, or at least started on the road to mastery, I will now call your attention to another important subject, that of mental leaks. No, I don't mean the leakage arising from your failure to keep your own secrets, the leakage I am referring to is that occasioned by the habit of having the attention attracted to and distracted by every passing fancy.

In order to attain a thing it is necessary that the mind should fall in love with it, and be conscious of its existence, almost to the exclusion of everything else. You must get in love with the thing you wish to attain, just as much as you would if you were to meet the girl or man you wished to marry. I do not mean that you should become a monomaniac upon the subject, and should lose all interest in everything else in the world, that won't do, for the mind must have recreation and change. But, I do mean that you must be so "set" upon the desired thing that all else will seem of secondary importance.

A man in love may be pleasant to every one else, and may go through the duties and pleasures of life with good spirit, but underneath it all he is humming to himself "Just One Girl;" and every one of his actions is bent toward getting that girl, and making a comfortable home for her. Do you see what I mean? You must get in love with the thing you want, and you must get in love with it in earnest, none of this latter-day flirting, "on-today and off-tomorrow" sort of love, but the good old-fashioned kind, that used to make it impossible for a young man to get to sleep unless he took a walk around his best girl's house, just to be sure it was still there. That's the real kind!

The man or woman in search of success must make of that desired thing his ruling passion - he must keep his mind on the main chance. Success is jealous, that's why we speak of her as feminine. She demands a man's whole affection, and if he begins flirting with other fair charmers, she soon turns her back upon him. If a man allows his strong interest in the main chance to be sidetracked, he will be the loser. Mental Force operates best when it is concentrated. You must give to the desired thing your best and most earnest thought. Just as the man who is thoroughly in love will think out plans and schemes whereby he may please the fair one, so will the man who is in love with his work or business give it his best thought, and the result will be that a hundred and one plans will come into his field of consciousness, many of which are very important.

The mind works on the subconscious plane, and almost always along the lines of the ruling passion or desire. It will fix up things, and patch together plans and schemes, and when you need them the most it will pop them into your consciousness, and you will feel just as if you had received some valuable aid from outside.

But if you scatter your thought-force, the subconscious mind will not know just how to please you, and the result is that you will be cut off from this source of aid and assistance. Beside this, you will miss the powerful result of concentrated thought in the conscious working out of the details of your plans.

The man whose mind is full of a dozen interests fails to exert the attracting power that is manifested by the man of the one ruling passion, and he fails to draw to him persons, things, and results that will aid in the working out of his plans, and will also fail to place himself in the current of attraction whereby he is brought into contact with those who will be glad to help him because of harmonious interests.

Love what you do

I have noticed, in my own affairs, that when I would allow myself to be side-tracked by anything outside of my regular line of work, it would be only a short time before my receipts dropped off, and my business showed signs of a lack of vitality.

Now, many may say that this was because I left undone some things that I would have done if my mind had been centered on the business. This is true; but I have noticed like results in cases where there was nothing to be done, cases in which the seed was sown, and the crop was awaited. In such cases, as soon as I directed my thought to the matter the seed began to sprout. I do not mean that I had to send out great mental waves with the idea of affecting people - not a bit of it. I simply began to realize what a good thing I had, and how much people wanted it, and how glad they would be to know of it, and all that sort of thing, and my thought seemed to vitalize the work, and the seed began to sprout. This is no mere fancy, for I have experienced it on several occasions; I have spoken to many others on the subject, and I find that our experiences tally perfectly. So don't get into the habit of permitting these mental leaks. Keep your Desire fresh and active, and let it get in its work without interference from conflicting desires.

Keep in love with the thing you wish to attain - feed your fancy with it - see it as accomplished already, but don't lose your interest. Keep your eye on the main prize, and keep your one ruling passion strong and vigorous. Don't be a mental polygamist - one mental love is all that a man needs - that is, one at a time.

Some scientists have claimed that something that might as well be called "Love" is at the bottom of the whole of life. They claim that the love of the plant for water causes it to send forth its roots until the loved thing is found. They say that the love of the flower for the sun causes it to grow away from the dark places, so that it may receive the light. These so-called "chemical affinities" are really a form of love, and Desire is a manifestation of this Universal Life Love. So I am not using a mere figure of speech when I tell you that you must love the thing you wish to attain. Nothing but intense love will enable you to surmount the many obstacles placed in your path. Nothing but that love will enable you to bear the burdens of the task. The more Desire you have for a thing, the more you Love it; and the more you Love it, the greater will be the attractive force exerted toward its attainment, both within yourself, and outside of you. So love but one thing at a time.

Chapter 13 Summary

• Avoid distractions, concentrate your mental force

• Fall in love with what you are doing and others will love it too

• We are attracted to what we love, and what we love is attracted to us

The Secret of Success

14

Successful vs. Unsuccessful

You have noticed the difference between the successful and strong men in any walk of life, and the unsuccessful weak men around them. You are conscious of the widely differing characteristics of the two classes, but find it difficult to determine just where the difference lies. Let us take a look at the matter.

Buxton said:

"The longer I live, the more certain I am that the great difference between men, the feeble and the powerful, the great and the insignificant, is energy and invincible determination-a purpose once fixed and then Death or Victory. That quality will do anything that can be done in this world - and no talents, no circumstances, no opportunities will make a two-legged creature a man without it."

I do not see how the idea could be more clearly expressed than Buxton has spoken. He has put his finger right in the center of the subject - his eye has seen into the heart of it.

Energy and determination

Energy and invincible determination - these two things will sweep away mighty barriers, and will surmount the greatest obstacles, and yet they must be used together. Energy without determination will go to waste. Lots of men have plenty of energy - they are full to overflowing with it; and yet they lack concentration - they lack the concentrated force that enables them to bring their power to bear upon the right spot.

Energy is not nearly so rare a thing as many imagine it to be. I can look around me at any time, and pick out a number of people I know who are full of energy - many of them are energy plus - and yet, somehow, they do not seem to make any headway. They are wasting their energy all the time. Now they are fooling with this thing-now meddling with that. They will take up some trifling thing of no real interest or importance, and waste enough energy and nervous force to carry them through a hard day's work; and yet when they are through, nothing has been accomplished.

Others who have plenty of energy, fail to direct it by the power of the Will toward the desired end. "Invincible determination" - those are the words. Do they not thrill you with their power? If you have something to do, get to work and do it. Marshal your energy, and then guide and direct it by your Will - bestow upon it that "invincible determination" and you will do the thing.

Everyone has within him a giant will, but the majority of us are too lazy to use it. We cannot get ourselves nerved up to the point at which we can say, truthfully: "I Will." If we can but screw up our courage to that point, and will then pin it in place so that it will not slip back, we will be able to call into play that wonderful power - the Human Will. Man, as a rule, has but the faintest conception of the power of the Will, but those who have studied along the occult teachings, know that the Will is one of the great dynamic forces of the universe, and if harnessed and directed properly it is capable of accomplishing almost miraculous things.

"Energy and Invincible Determination"- aren't they magnificent words? Commit them to memory - press them like a die into the wax of your mind, and they will be a constant inspiration to you in hours of need. If you can get these words to vibrating in your being, you will be a giant among pygmies. Say these words over and over again, and see how you are filled with new life - see how your blood will circulate - how your nerves will tingle. Make these words a part of yourself, and then go forth anew to the battle of life, encouraged and strengthened. Put them into practice. "Energy and Invincible Determination"- let that be your motto in your work-a-day life, and you will be one of those rare men who are able to "do things."

Many persons are deterred from doing their best by the fact that they underrate themselves by comparison with the successful ones of life, or rather, they overrate the successful ones by comparison with themselves.

Successful people aren't extraordinary

One of the curious things noticed by those who are brought in contact with the people who have "arrived" is the fact that these successful people are not extraordinary after all. You meet with some great writer, and you are disappointed to find him very ordinary indeed. He does not converse brilliantly, and, in fact, you know a score of everyday people who seem far more brilliant than this man who dazzles you by his brightness in his books. You meet some great statesman, and he does not seem nearly as wise as lots of old fellows in your own village, who waste their wisdom upon the desert air. You meet some great captain of industry, and he does not give you the impression of the shrewdness so marked in some little bargain-driving trader in your own town. How is this, anyway? Are the reputations of these people fictitious, or what is the trouble?

The trouble is this: You have imagined these people to be made of superior metal, and are disappointed to find them made of the same stuff as yourself and those about you. But, you ask, wherein does their greatness of achievement lie? Chiefly in this: Belief in themselves and in their inherent power, in their faculty to concentrate on the work in hand, when they are working, and in their ability to prevent leaks of power when they are not working. They believe in themselves, and make every effort count.

Your village wise man spills his wisdom on every corner, and talks to a lot of fools; when if he really were wise he would save up his wisdom and place it where it would do some work. The brilliant writer does not waste his wit upon every comer; in fact, he shuts the drawer in which he contains his wit, and opens it only when he is ready to concentrate and get down to business.

The captain of industry has no desire to impress you with his shrewdness and "smartness." He never did, even when he was young. While his companions were talking and boasting, and "blowing," this future successful financier was "sawin" wood and sayin nuthin."

Successful people are not very different from you

The great people of the world - that is, those who have "arrived"- are not very different from you, or me, or the rest of us - all of us are about the same at the base. You have only to meet them to see how very "ordinary" they are, after all. But, don't forget the fact that they know how to use the material that is in them; while the rest of the crowd does not, and, in fact, even doubts whether the true stuff is there.

The man or woman who "gets there," usually starts out by realizing that he or she is not so very different, after all, from the successful people that they hear so much about. This gives them confidence, and the result is they find out that they are able to "do things." Then they learn to keep their mouths closed, and to avoid wasting and dissipating their energy. They store up energy, and concentrate it upon the task at hand; while their companions are scattering their energies in every direction, trying to show off and let people know how smart they are. The man or woman who "gets there," prefers to wait for the applause that follows deeds accomplished, and cares very little for the praise that attends promises of what we expect to do "some day," or an exhibition of "smartness" without works.

Success is contagious

One of the reasons that people who are thrown in with successful men often manifest success themselves, is that they are able to watch the successful man and sort of "catch the trick" of his greatness. They see that he is an everyday sort of man, but that he thoroughly believes in himself, and also that he does not waste energy, but reserves all his force for the actual tasks before him. And, profiting by example, they start to work and put the lesson into practice in their own lives.

Now what is the moral of this talk? Simply this: Don't undervalue yourself, or overvalue others. Realize that you are made of good stuff, and that locked within your mind are many good things. Then get to work and unfold those good things, and make something out of that good stuff. Do this by attention to the things before you, and by giving to each the best that is in you, knowing that plenty of more good things are in you ready for the fresh tasks that will come. Put the best of yourself into the undertaking on hand, and do not cheat the present task in favor of some future one. Your supply is inexhaustible. And don't waste your good stuff on the crowd of gapers, watchers and critics who are standing around watching you work. Save your good stuff for your job, and don't be in too much of a hurry for applause. Save up your good thoughts for "copy" if you are a writer; save up your bright schemes for actual practice, if you are a business man; save up your wisdom for occasion, if you are a statesman; and, in each case, avoid the desire to scatter your pearls before - well, before the gaping crowd that wants to be entertained by a "free show."

Nothing very "high" about this teaching, perhaps, but it is what many of you need very much.

Stop fooling around, and get down to business. Stop wasting good raw material, and start to work making something worthwhile.

Chapter 14 Summary

• Energy and determination are the keys to success

• Successful people are not that different from you

• Do not undervalue yourself or others

• Success is contagious, if you associate with successful people

• Don't waste your energy

• "I Can and I Will"

"The strongest single factor in prosperity consciousness is self-esteem: believing you can do it, believing you deserve it, believing you will get it."

Jerry Gillies

You Are Entitled

15

Nothing is too good for you

In a recent conversation, I was telling a woman to pluck up courage and to reach out for a certain good thing for which she had been longing for many years, and which, at last, appeared to be in sight. I told her that it looked as if her desire was about to be gratified - that the Law of Attraction was bringing it to her. She lacked faith, and kept on repeating, "Oh! It's too good to be true - it's too good for me!" She had not emerged from the worm-of-the-dust stage, and although she was in sight of the Promised Land she refused to enter it because it "was too good for her." I think I succeeded in putting sufficient "ginger" into her to enable her to claim her own, for the last reports indicate that she is taking possession.

Ask for what you want

But that is not what I wish to tell you. I want to call your attention to the fact that nothing is too good for you - no matter how great the thing may be - no matter how undeserving you may seem to be. You are entitled to the best there is, for it is your direct inheritance. So don't be afraid to ask, demand, and take. The good things of the world are not the portion of any favored sons. They belong to all, but they come only to those who are wise enough to recognize that the good things are theirs by right, and who are sufficiently courageous to reach out for them. Many good things are lost for want of the asking. Many splendid things are lost to you because of your feeling that you are unworthy of them. Many great things are lost to you because you lack the confidence and courage to demand and take possession of them.

"None but the brave deserves the fair," says the old adage, and the rule is true in all lines of human effort. If you keep on repeating that you are unworthy of the good thing, that it is too good for you, the Law will be apt to take you at your word and believe what you say. That's a peculiar thing about the Law, it believes what you say, it takes you in earnest. So beware what you say to it, for it will be apt to give credence. Say to it that you are worthy of the best there is, and that there is nothing too good for you, and you will be likely to have the Law take you in earnest, and say, "I guess he is right; I'm going to give him the whole bakeshop if he wants it, he knows his rights, and what's the use of trying to deny it to him?" But if you say, "Oh, it's too good for me!" the Law will probably say, "Well, I wouldn't wonder but what that is so. Surely he ought to know, and it isn't for me to contradict him." And so it goes.

Why should anything be too good for you? Did you ever stop to think just what you are? You are a manifestation of the Whole Thing, and have a perfect right to all there is. Or, if you prefer it this way, you are a child of the Infinite, and are heir to it all. You are telling the truth in either statement, or both. At any rate, no matter for what you ask, you are merely demanding your own. The more in earnest you are about demanding it - the more confident you are of receiving it - the more will you use in reaching out for it - the surer you will be to obtain it.

Strong desire - confident expectation - courage in action - these things bring to you your own. But before you put these forces into effect, you must awaken to a realization that you are merely asking for your own, and not for something to which you have no right or claim. So long as there exists in your mind the last sneaking bit of doubt as to your right to the things you want, you will be setting up a resistance to the operation of the Law. You may demand as vigorously as you please, but you will lack the courage to act if you have a lingering doubt of your right to the thing you want. If you persist in regarding the desired thing as if it belonged to another, instead of to yourself, you will be placing yourself in the position of the covetous or envious man, or even in the position of a tempted thief. In such a case your mind will revolt at proceeding with the work, for it instinctively will recoil from the idea of taking what is not your own - the mind is honest. But when you realize that the best the Universe holds belongs to you as a Divine Heir, and that there is enough for all without your robbing anyone else; then the friction is removed, and the barrier broken down, and the Law proceeds to do its work.

I do not believe in this "humble" business. This meek and lowly attitude does not appeal to me -there is no sense in it, at all. The idea of making a virtue of such things, when Man is the heir of the Universe, and is entitled to whatever he needs for his growth, happiness and satisfaction! I do not mean that one should assume a blustering and domineering attitude of mind - that is also absurd, for true strength does not exhibit itself. The blusterer is a self-confessed weakling - he blusters to disguise his weakness. The truly strong man is calm, self-contained, and carries with him a consciousness of strength which renders unnecessary the bluster and fuss of assumed strength. But get away from this hypnotism of "humility" - this "meek and lowly" attitude of mind. Remember the horrible example of Uriah Heep, and beware of imitating him. Throw back your head, and look the world square in the face. There's nothing to be afraid of - the world is apt to be as much afraid of you, as you are of it, anyway. Be a man, or woman, and not a crawling thing. This applies to your mental attitude, as well as to your outward demeanor. Stop this crawling in your mind. See yourself as standing erect and facing life without fear, and you will gradually grow into your ideal.

Who is Uriah Heep?

Uriah Heep is a fictional character in the novel David Copperfield by Charles Dickens. Atkinson is warning against the kind of fake humility, and insincere flattery that this character exhibited in the book.

You are a child of the Emperor

There is nothing that is too good for you - not a thing. The best there is, is not beginning to be good enough for you; for there are still better things ahead. The best gift that the world has to offer is a mere bauble compared to the great things in the Cosmos that await your coming of age. So don't be afraid to reach out for these playthings of life - these baubles of this plane of consciousness. Reach out for them - grab a whole fistful - play with them until you are tired; that's what they are made for, anyway.

They are made for our express use - not to look at, but to be played with, if you desire. Help yourself-there's a whole shop full of these toys awaiting your desire, demand and taking. Don't be bashful! Don't let me hear any more of this silly talk about things being too good for you. You have been like the Emperor's little son thinking that the tin soldiers and toy drum were far too good for him, and refusing to reach out for them. But you don't find this trouble with children as a rule. They instinctively recognize that nothing is too good for them. They want all that is in sight to play with, and they seem to feel that the things are theirs by right. That is the condition of mind that we seekers after the Divine Adventure must cultivate. Unless we become as little children we cannot enter the Kingdom of Heaven.

The things we see around us are the playthings of the Kindergarten of God, playthings which we use in our game-tasks. Help yourself to them - ask for them without bashfulness - demand as many as you can make use of - for they are yours. If you don't see just exactly what you want, ask for it - there's a big reserve stock on the shelves, and in the closets. Play, play, play, to your heart's content. Learn to weave mats - to build houses with the blocks - to stitch outlines on the squares - play the game through, and play it well. Demand all the proper materials for the play - don't be bashful - there's enough to go round.

Life is a game

But, remember this, while all this be true, the best things are still only game-things - toys, blocks, mats, cubes, and all the rest. Useful, most useful for the learning of the lessons - pleasant, most pleasant with which to play - and desirable, most desirable, for these purposes. Get all the fun and profit out of the use of things that is possible. Throw yourself heartily into the game, and play it out - it is Good. But, here's the thing to remember - never lose sight of the fact that these good things are but playthings - part of the game - and you must be perfectly willing to lay them aside when the time comes to pass into the next class, and not cry and mourn because you must leave your playthings behind you. Do not allow yourself to become unduly attached to them - they are for your use and pleasure, but are not a part of you - not essential to your happiness in the next stage. Despise them not because of their lack of Reality - they are great things relatively, and you may as well have all the fun out of them that you can - don't be a spiritual prig, standing aside and refusing to join in the game. But do not tie yourself to them - they are good to use and play with, but not good enough to use you and to make you a plaything. Don't let the toys turn the tables on you.

This is the difference between the Master of Circumstances and the Slave of Circumstances. The Slave thinks that these playthings are real, and that he is not good enough to have them. He gets only a few toys, because he is afraid to ask for more, and he misses most of the fun. Then, considering the toys to be real, and not realizing that there are plenty more where these came from, he attaches himself to the little trinkets that have come his way, and allows himself to be made a slave of them. He is afraid that they may be taken away from him, and he is afraid to toddle across the floor and help himself to the others.

The Master knows that all are his for the asking. He demands that which he needs from day to day, and does not worry about overloading himself; for he knows that there are "lots more," and that he cannot be cheated out of them. He plays, and plays well, and has a good time in the play-and he learns his Kindergarten lessons in the playing. But he does not become too much attached to his toys. He is willing to fling away the worn-out one, and reach out for a new one. When he is called into the next room for promotion, he drops on the floor the worn-out toys of the day, and with glistening eyes and confident attitude of mind, marches into the next room - into the Great Unknown - with a smile on his face. He is not afraid, for he hears the voice of the Teacher, and knows that she is there waiting for him - in that Great Next Room.

Chapter 15 Summary

- Nothing is too good for you

- Ask for what you want

- If you say that something is too good for you the universe will take you at your word

- Life is a game, have fun, but don't get too attached to your toys

"Luck is what happens when preparation meets opportunity."

Seneca
(Roman philosopher 1st century AD)

16

Law, Not Chance

Luck?

Some time ago I was talking to a man about the Attractive Power of Thought. He said that he did not believe that Thought could attract anything to him, and that it was all a matter of luck. He had found, he said, that ill luck relentlessly pursued him, and that everything he touched went wrong. It always had, and always would, and he had grown to expect it. When he undertook a new thing he knew beforehand that it would go wrong and that no good would come of it. Oh, no, there wasn't anything in the theory of Attractive Thought, so far as he could see; it was all a matter of luck!

This man failed to see that by his own confession he was giving a most convincing argument in favor of the Law of Attraction. He was testifying that he was always expecting things to go wrong, and that they always came about as he expected. He was a magnificent illustration of the Law of Attraction - but he didn't know it, and no argument seemed to make the matter clear to him. He was "up against it," and there was no way out of it - he always expected the ill luck, and every occurrence proved that he was right, and that the Mental Science position was all nonsense.

Belief

There are many people who seem to think that the only way in which the Law of Attraction operates is when one wishes hard, strong and steady. They do not seem to realize that a strong belief is as efficacious as a strong wish. The successful man believes in himself and in his ultimate success, and, paying no attention to little setbacks, stumbles, tumbles and slips, presses on eagerly to the goal, believing all the time that he will get there. His views and aims may alter as he progresses, and he may change his plans or have them changed for him, but all the time he knows in his heart that he will eventually "get there." He is not steadily wishing he may get there - he simply feels it and believes it, and thereby sets into operation the strongest forces known in the world of thought.

The man who just as steadily believes he is going to fail will invariably fail. How could he help it? There is no special miracle about it. Everything he does, thinks and says is tinctured with the thought of failure. Other people catch his spirit, and fail to trust him or his ability, which occurrences he in turn sets down as but other exhibitions of his ill luck, instead of ascribing them to his belief and expectation of failure. He is suggesting failure to himself all the time, and he invariably takes on the effect of the autosuggestion. Then, again, he by his negative thoughts shuts up that portion of his mind from which should come the ideas and plans conducive to success and which do come to the man who is expecting success because he believes in it. A state of discouragement is not the one in which bright ideas come to us. It is only when we are enthused and hopeful that our minds work out the bright ideas which we may turn to account.

Men instinctively feel the atmosphere of failure hovering around certain of their fellows, and on the other hand recognize something about others which leads them to say, when they hear of a temporary mishap befalling such a one: "Oh, he'll come out all right somehow - you can't keep him down." It is the atmosphere caused by the prevailing Mental Attitude. So, clear up your Mental Atmosphere!

There is no such thing as chance. Law maintains everywhere, and all that happens, happens because of the operation of Law. You cannot name the simplest thing that ever occurred by chance - try it, and then run the thing down to a final analysis, and you will see it as the result of Law. It is as plain as mathematics. Plan and purpose; cause and effect. From the movements of worlds to the growth of the grain of mustard seed - all are the result of Law. The fall of the stone down the mountain-side is not chance - forces which had been in operation for centuries caused it. Back of that cause were other causes, and so on until the Causeless Cause is reached.

Life is not the result of chance - the Law is here, too. The Law is in full operation whether you know it or not - whether you believe in it or not. You may be the ignorant object upon which the Law operates, and bring yourself all sorts of trouble because of your ignorance of or opposition to the Law. Or you may fall in with the operations of the Law - get into its current - and Life will seem a far different thing to you. You cannot get outside of the Law, by refusing to have anything to do with it. You are at liberty to oppose it and produce all the friction you wish to - it doesn't hurt the Law, and you may keep it up until you learn your lesson.

The Law of Thought Attraction is one name for the Law, or rather for one manifestation of it. Again I say, your thoughts are real things. They go forth from you in all directions, combining with thoughts of like kind - opposing thoughts of a different character - forming combinations - going where they are attracted - flying away from thought centers opposing them. Your mind attracts the thoughts of others, which have been sent out by them consciously or unconsciously. But it attracts only those thoughts which are in harmony with its own. Like attracts like, and opposites repel opposites in the world of thought.

Set your mind to the frequency of success

If you set your mind to the frequency of courage, confidence, strength and success, you attract to yourself thoughts of like nature; people of like nature; things that fit in the mental tune. Your prevailing thought or mood determines that which is to be drawn toward you - it picks out your mental bedfellow. You are today setting into motion thought currents which will in time attract toward you thoughts, people and conditions in harmony with the predominant note of your thought. Your thought will mingle with that of others of like nature and mind, and you will be attracted toward each other, and will surely come together with a common purpose sooner or later, unless one or the other of you should change the current of his thoughts.

Fall in with the operations of the Law. Make it a part of yourself. Get into its currents. Maintain your poise. Set your mind to the frequency of courage, confidence and success. Get in touch with all the thoughts of that kind that are emanating every hour from hundreds of minds. Get the best that is to be had in the thought world. The best is there, so be satisfied with nothing less. Get into partnership with good minds. Get into the right vibrations. You must be tired of being tossed about by the operations of the Law - get into harmony with it.

Chapter 16 Summary

• There is no such thing as luck,
if you believe something will happen it will because you will put in the necessary time and effort and attract the thing to you

• You can set your mind to the frequency of courage, confidence, strength, and success

Appendix A - What I Believe

My Working Creed

• I believe that the mind of Man contains the greatest of all forces and that Thought is one of the greatest manifestations of energy.

• I believe that the man who understands the use of Thought-force can make of himself practically what he will.

• I believe that not only is one's body subject to the control of the mind, but that, also, one may change environment, luck, and circumstances, by positive thought taking the place of negative. I know that the **"I Can and I Will"** attitude will carry one forward to Success that will seem miraculous to the man on the "I Can't" plane.

• I believe that **"thoughts are things,"** and that the Law of Attraction in the thought world will draw to one just what he desires or fears.

• **I believe in the gospel of work**, I believe in "hustling."

• I believe in the **"I DO,"** as well as the **"I AM."** I know that the man who will take advantage of the Power of the Mind, and who will manifest that power in action, will go forward to Success as surely and as steadily as the arrow from the bow of the skilled archer.

• I believe in the **Brotherhood of Man.**

• I believe in being **Kind.**

• I believe in everyone minding his own business - and allowing everyone else the same privilege. I believe that **we have no right to condemn** -"let him who is without sin cast the first stone."

• I believe that he who Hates is an assassin; that he who Covets is a thief; that he who Lusts is an adulterer; that **the gist of a crime is in its desire.** Seeing this - looking into our own hearts - how can we condemn?

• I believe that **Evil is but Ignorance.**

• I believe that **"to know all is to forgive all."**

• I believe that **there is good in every man;** let us help him to manifest it.

• I believe in the absolute **equality of the Man and the Woman** - sometimes I think that the odds are slightly in favor of the Woman.

• I believe in the sacredness of Sex - but I also believe that Sex manifests on the Spiritual and Mental planes as well as on the Physical. I believe that to the pure all things are pure.

• I believe that **man is immortal** - that the Real Self is Spirit, which uses mind and body as its tools, and manifests itself according to the fitness of the tools.

• I believe that Man is rapidly growing into a new plane of consciousness, in which he will know himself as he is - will recognize the "I AM" - the Something Within.

• I believe that there is an Infinite Power in, and of, all things.

• I believe that, although today we have but the faintest idea of that Power, still we will steadily grow to comprehend it more fully - will get in closer touch with it. Even now we have momentary glimpses of its existence - a momentary consciousness of

Oneness with the Absolute.

• I believe that the greatest happiness consists in maintaining toward the Absolute the attitude of the trusting child, who, feeling no doubt of the parent's love - no doubt of his wisdom - places his little hand in that of the parent, and says "Lead Thou me on."

• I believe that he who feels towards the Absolute, the trustfulness of the babe which places its little tired head close to the breast of the mother, will also be conscious of the tender answering pressure, as the babe is drawn just a little closer to the mother-heart.

William Walker Atkinson

Appendix B

Who was William Walker Atkinson?

William Walker Atkinson was an author, publisher, and lawyer who was actively involved with the emerging New Thought movement of the 1880's.

He was born in Baltimore, Maryland on December 5, 1862. His father was a grocer and his early years were spent helping in the family business. He went on to practice law in Pennsylvania and later in Illinois.

He became involved in the New Thought movement as a result of a physical and mental breakdown due to business and financial stress while in his 20's. He attributed the recovery of both his health and his financial situation to the application of the ideas and principles of New Thought.

Atkinson moved to Chicago in the late 1890's

and began publishing New Thought magazines and literature such as "Suggestion," "New Thought," and "Advanced Thought" in addition to practicing law.

A prolific author

He became a prolific author, but it is not known for certain how many books he actually wrote since many of his books were written under various pseudonyms. Close to one hundred books have been confirmed as having been written by him, but there are believed to be many more that have not been identified. Some of the names he wrote under include: Theodore Sheldon, Theron Q. Dumont, Swami Panchadasi, The Three Initiates, and Magus Incognitus.

In addition to New Thought and personal development, Atkinson studied Hinduism and Yoga and wrote numerous books and articles on these subjects and was instrumental in introducing eastern concepts such as Karma and Reincarnation into western thought.

Unanswered questions

William Walker Atkinson died on November 22, 1932, in Los Angeles, California and left behind several unanswered questions, not the least of which was **"Why so many pseudonyms?"** It has been suggested that he chose to write under pseudonyms in order to protect his successful law career, but I think that is unlikely. He never shied away from exposing his somewhat unorthodox beliefs when he was writing under his own name.

Another unanswered question was, **"Did his co-authors actually exist?"** He apparently co-authored books with Edward Beals and William De Laurence, but even this is uncertain.

"Was he simply a shrewd businessman who realized that he would sell more books if people believed that he was someone else?" This is possible. When he wrote under the names Swami Panchadasi and Yogi Ramacharaka he claimed to be a Hindu. When he wrote under the name of Theron Q. Dumont he claimed to be an Instructor on the Art and Science of Personal Magnetism, living in Paris, France.

However, it is also possible that these were actual people and that he wrote the books on their behalf like as a ghost writer would. We will probably never know for sure.

His words speak for themselves

But regardless of what the actual answers to these questions are, even after all these years, his words speak for themselves. Follow the advice he gives in the introduction to this book, don't follow him! But, if anything he said strikes a chord with you, if there is something in his writing that benefits you, then take it and use it to your benefit.

Irene McGarvie
Toronto, ON
2011

Appendix C

What is the "New Thought" Movement?

New Thought has been referred to as the "Mind Cure" movement because of the premise that our bodies are under the control of our minds, but it is about much more than just healing the physical body. The New Thought movement is a spiritual movement that began in the late 1800's and which emphasizes the belief that God, or Infinite Intelligence is everywhere and in everyone, that we are eternal spiritual beings currently inhabiting a physical body, and that we create our own happiness or unhappiness through our thoughts and actions. It stresses that the knowledge of spiritual principles is not enough, but that we must actually live the principles in order to benefit from them.

New Thought is the basis of much of the New Age and self-help teachings such as *"The Secret."*

One of the main premises of New Thought is that it is continually evolving. As mankind learns more about how the universe works New Thought itself will evolve to incorporate the new information.

The ideas presented in New Thought are not new. Great minds throughout history including Socrates, Aristotle, and the Buddha have all advocated many of these same ideas.

New Thought today

New Thought has influenced much of our present day spiritual beliefs even within traditional Christian Churches, but there are a few religious organizations that are particularly associated with New Thought. These include Unity Church, Religious Science or Science of Mind, The Church of Divine Science, as well as numerous smaller off-shoots of these groups. While not exactly "Christian" they emphasize the New Testament teachings of Jesus as a philosophy.

An explosion of self-help books

New Thought authors in the 1890's and early 20th century are largely responsible for the development of the "self-help" book genre. In addition to William Walker Atkinson some early New Thought authors include:

> James Allen
> Ella Wheeler Wilcox
> Bruce MacLelland
> Wallace Wattles
> Florence Scovel Shinn
> Phineas P. Quimby
> Prentice Mulford
> Ernest Holmes
> Napoleon Hill
> Robert Collier
> Charles Filmore
> Ralph Waldo Emerson

Some highly recommended modern New Thought authors include Eric Butterworth and Catherine Ponder.

*"You are what you think,
not what you think you are."*

Bruce MacLelland
(Author of *"Prosperity Through Thought Force"*)

More Books of Ancient Wisdom

The Sweat Lodge is For Everyone

ISBN 978-0-9737470-6-5 $19.95

The Native American Sweat Lodge Ceremony offers so many benefits, both spiritual and physical for anyone who has the opportunity to take part in one.

This book is the non-Native's guide to understanding, participating in, and benefiting from Native American Sweat Lodge ceremonies.

Messages in Your Tea Cup

ISBN 978-0-9783939-6-0 $19.95

Have you ever wished that you could predict the future? Throughout history people all over the world have been able to predict future events and get advice from "beyond" through tea leaf reading.

This book will teach you everything that you need to know to begin reading tea leaves immediately.

More Books of Ancient Wisdom

Séances in Washington

Séances in Washington:
Abraham Lincoln and Spiritualism during the Civil War

Nettie Colburn Maynard

ISBN 978-0-9783939-7-7 $19.95

Abraham Lincoln and Spiritualism during the Civil War. This book is the first-hand account of the experiences of a Spiritualist medium in Washington during the Civil War. It created tremendous controversy when it was originally published in 1891, but there were enough credible witnesses to confirm her account of events that it could not be disputed.

The Spirituality of Money

The Spirituality of Money

Your mistaken beliefs about money could be preventing you from living the life you deserve

Mike Morley & Irene McGarvie

ISBN 978-0-9783939-3-9 $9.95

Does it feel like money is a constant struggle for you? We keep hearing about how easy it is to "manifest" anything we want, including money, but for most people it just isn't that easy.

This book will help you recognize the false beliefs about money that are keeping you from living the life of abundance that you deserve.

More Books of Ancient Wisdom

Pious Fraud

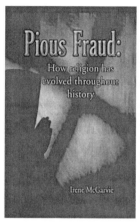

ISBN 978-0-9783939-7-7 $19.95

This book shows how all of our present day western religious beliefs came from one early form of religion, and how religious leaders throughout history have adapted these religious beliefs to control their followers. Discover how the literal "truths" and "historical events" of the Bible were actually based on ancient pagan solar worship.

Mirror Gazing

ISBN 978-1-926826-01-1 $19.95

Predict the future, look into the past, unlock your creativity. Scrying, is a technique that anyone can use to access information previously hidden from your conscious awareness. For centuries churches have condemned mirror gazing as satanic or evil, and yet many Bible figures used a form of it to receive Divine guidance. So which is it, a useful skill or a demonic tool?

More Books of Ancient Wisdom

The Future is in Your Hands

ISBN 978-0-9783939-8-4 $19.95

Palm Reading Made Easy

It is uncanny, but palmistry really works! This book teaches how to predict the future and understand yourself and others through studying the lines on the palm of the hand (palm reading - cheiromancy) and studying the shape of the hand and fingers (hand reading - cheirognomy).

Timeless Love

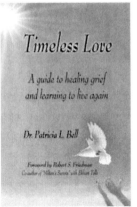

ISBN 978-0-9783939-9-1 $14.95

Timeless Love is a guide to healing grief and learning to live again. By looking at the unique relationship between the reader and the person who has passed this book explains how these losses affect each person differently. The reader is then guided into healing the grief and rebuilding their life.

CPSIA information can be obtained
at www.ICGtesting.com
Printed in the USA
FFOW05n1739260615

9 781926 826035